CAMBRIDGE STUDIES IN LINGUISTICS

Linguistic Realities

In this series

Supplementary volumes

Earlier titles not listed are also available
*Issued in hard covers and as a paperback

LINGUISTIC REALITIES
AN AUTONOMIST METATHEORY
FOR THE GENERATIVE ENTERPRISE

PHILIP CARR

English Language Department
University of Newcastle upon Tyne

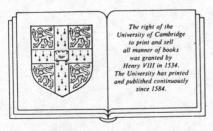

The right of the
University of Cambridge
to print and sell
all manner of books
was granted by
Henry VIII in 1534.
The University has printed
and published continuously
since 1584.

CAMBRIDGE UNIVERSITY PRESS

CAMBRIDGE

NEW YORK   PORT CHESTER

MELBOURNE   SYDNEY

Published by the Press Syndicate of the University of Cambridge
The Pitt Building, Trumpington Street, Cambridge CB2 1RP
40 West 20th Street, New York, NY 10011, USA
10 Stamford Road, Oakleigh, Melbourne 3166, Australia

First published 1990

Printed in Great Britain at the University Press, Cambridge

British Library cataloguing in publication data
Carr, Philip
Linguistic realities: an autonomist meta-
theory for the generative enterprise.
(Cambridge studies in linguistics; 53)
1. Generative linguistics
I. Title
415

Library of Congress cataloguing in publication data
Carr, Philip, 1953–
Linguistic realities: an autonomist metatheory for
the generative enterprise / Philip Carr.
p.   cm. – (Cambridge studies in linguistics: 53)
Includes index.
ISBN 0-521-36401-9
1. Linguistics—Methodology.   I. Title.   II. Series.
P126.C37   1990
410′. 1—DC20
89-33197
CIP

ISBN 0 521 36401 9

EA

For my mother, and Lucy

Contents

Acknowledgements

This book is a revised version of my 1987 Edinburgh University doctoral thesis, 'Instrumentalism, realism, and the object of inquiry in theoretical linguistics'. It was Roger Lass, my supervisor in the early stages of the thesis, whose lively classes first aroused my curiosity in issues in the philosophy of science, and their consequences for linguistics. I am indebted to him for having done so. I am also grateful to Jim Hurford, who supervised the bulk of the thesis with immensely encouraging interest and responsiveness. Both of them possess the quality of being able to take their students seriously; for this I thank them.

Hans-Heinrich Lieb very kindly read the thesis in considerable detail. My thanks to him for this and for his probing, insightful questions; had I encountered his work earlier, I might have saved myself a great deal of difficulty. Esa Itkonen has responded readily to my queries about his work with great care and patience; I hope he does not feel that I have done him any injustice in my exposition of his views.

I am fortunate to have had Noël Burton-Roberts as a colleague for the past five years. I thank him for many discussions on matters metatheoretical; his undying sense of wonder has made it all enormously enjoyable. Arleta Adamska-Sałaciak has provided thought-provoking comments on abduction and analogy for quite some time; many thanks to her for putting up with me.

I am also grateful to audiences in universities in England, Poland, and Scotland for their responses to my oral presentations of my thoughts on linguistic metatheory, and to my examiners, Geoffrey Sampson and Ronnie Cann. Thanks too to Jim Crabb, who came to the rescue at the last minute with some valuable proof-reading. I am lucky to have had extra-curricular encouragement from Adrian Ribolla, at Acanthus, and Clive Walton, in the Covenanter; they have both helped considerably. Without Hermann Moisl, I would probably still be using a manual typewriter. Finally, I thank Inès, for the ineffable.

Introduction

Can we reasonably speak of 'linguistic realities'? To make any headway in responding to this question, we must tackle several rather complex issues in the philosophy of linguistics concerning the nature and object of linguistic theorising. This book is an attempt to unpack those issues and to provide an answer to the question – in the affirmative. In providing this answer, I will be tackling two closely related issues, which I will refer to as the 'methodological question' and the 'ontological question'.

The first of these, which I address in part I, may be posed thus: do theoretical linguists devise accounts of a reality which exists outside of their theories? In order to shed some light on what an answer to the methodological question might look like, part I investigates what is known as the realist/instrumentalist debate in the philosophy of science and shows what relevance it has for the sorts of question linguists might ask themselves about the nature of the discipline they are engaged in. It should be stressed that none of the material in part I is intended as an attempt at a contribution to the debates on these issues in the philosophy of science; the aim, rather, is to use the sorts of distinction made by philosophers of science (notably Popper) to elucidate the nature of theorising in theoretical linguistics. I do not assume any familiarity on the part of the reader with the (extensive) philosophy of science literature, one of the aims of the book being to introduce linguists to that literature.

I think that a brief (and necessarily over-simplified) outline of realist and instrumentalist positions in the philosophy of science is in order at this point. A realist view of theoretical constructs in science may be stated thus: such constructs may refer to, or be descriptive of, extra-theoretical realities. In this respect, the realist may wish to distinguish the following: (1) theory construction, (2) observable phenomena or sense data, and (3) a 'hidden' reality 'behind' these sense impressions, a reality which induces them. The task of the realist is then to devise, with the aid of (2), theoretical constructs in (1) which are descriptive of the reality in (3). The realist wants to claim for the propositions expressed as sentences containing his theoretical terms that they are potentially false, and thus informative, descriptions of a reality which underlies the phenomena. If we allow that generalisations about a domain of inquiry can be expressed by showing that a range of phenomena follow from (stronger still, are caused by) some (law-like, or other) property of the underlying reality, then we can claim to have achieved an explanation of those phenomena.

Since there are many different versions of realism in the philosophy of science, it is necessary to describe the different philosophical strands that usually function as components of realism. To do this, I will give an outline of Popper's versions of realism, as exemplified in his (1959) *Logic of Scientific Discovery*, in the (1963) collection of papers entitled *Conjectures and Refutations*, and in the three-volume (1982/3) *Postscript to the logic of Scientific Discovery*, at the same time discussing some of the problems it faces.

The instrumentalist view might be put as follows: it is a mistake to take theoretical constructs as being descriptive of some 'hidden reality' over and above the observable data. Rather, they are best seen as instruments for systematising, imposing order on, and predicting our sense impressions (or 'observable phenomena'). Propositions expressed as sentences which contain theoretical terms are neither true nor false, since our theoretical terms are not observational terms but are tools, and nothing more than tools, for the ordering and predicting of observations. Theoretical terms cannot be used to refer to 'real' entities; the entities which we may say they are used to refer to are fictitious objects which we devise in order to predict the phenomena.

This rather simplistic summary of the instrumentalist and realist positions should suffice to set the context for the discussions in part I, in which I will attempt to sustain a version of a realist philosophy of linguistics, starting with an outline of Popper's realism and defending it in the light of problems raised by what has been called the instrumentalist challenge to realism.

The ontological question, the subject matter of part II, could be put as follows: if we can reasonably speak of an extra-theoretical reality to which grammatical theories are directed, what sort of reality might that be? Here we return to the opening question, which can be posed in this way: are there specifically *linguistic* realities which constitute something over and above the objects of social and psychological theory? My task will be to show that it is reasonable to say that there are, since this affirmative answer runs counter to the version of psychologism which is probably still held by the majority of linguists. Psychologism is the view consistently defended by Chomsky over a rather long period (1968, 1975, 1986), that linguistic objects and states of affairs are speaker-internal and thus that theoretical linguistics is in some sense a branch of cognitive psychology. Chomsky's position entails a denial of the possibility of autonomism, which consists of the thesis that there are linguistic objects which are inadequately described as being social and/or psychological in nature, coupled with the thesis that grammatical inquiry is a discipline distinct in method and evidence from social and psychological theory.

With the appearance of Itkonen's (1978) work on the status of linguistic knowledge as socially established mutual knowledge and Katz's (1981) arguments for a Platonist ontology, psychologism came to be faced with serious challenges, and autonomism began to be advocated. Part II thus sets out to consider the competing positions available to us in response to the ontological question, to show what problems are raised for these, and to sustain an ontology which maintains that linguistic states of affairs are most appropriately described under something like Popper's (1972) notion of objective knowledge.

This combination of realism and an objectivist ontology constitutes a distinct, and very Popperian, metatheory, which I refer to as interaction-ism, following Popper. There are, of course, a great many problems facing Popper's positions on these matters, and a rather large amount of critical work available on his ideas. Many of the criticisms levelled at his philosophy of science could have been obviated had the *Postscript to the Logic of Scientific Discovery*, containing Popper's replies to his critics, been published in the 1950s when it was written. Unfortunately this work was not published until 1982/3; it shows rather clearly that much of the criticism of Popper's remarks on method in science is misguided in that it has been directed against views he has never held. The same cannot be said of the criticism of his more recent work on the ontology of scientific knowledge, some of the difficulties of which I try to deal with below. The aim of this work is not to pursue these difficulties at length, however, but to see what use these ideas can be put to in answering questions on linguistic meta-theory. If, by the end of part II, I have not succeeded in persuading the reader that this interactionist metatheory is on the right lines, I hope at least to have given the issues an airing, and to have pointed out some fundamental difficulties which have been inherent in the psychological realism assumed by theoretical linguists for more than two decades.

I should add, finally, that the division between matters methodological and ontological is rather artificial, as will soon emerge; one cannot first establish whether we are dealing with an extra-theoretical reality and then proceed to ask what its ontology might be. However, the division will suffice as a means of sorting out the issues which arise when we set out to establish what sort of enterprise theoretical linguistics is.

I

THE METHODOLOGICAL QUESTION

1   *The case for realism*

1.1   Science and realism

If we are to make any sense of the matter of whether theoretical linguistics is a science, then we must address the question of what sorts of activity could be said to count as sciences; hence the importance to linguistics of the issues discussed by philosophers of science. Any such discussion is meaningless unless we allow that there is a distinction to be made between scientific and non-scientific theories and the knowledge they allow us. Everything I say here will therefore presuppose that with the emergence of Western science a new kind of method of addressing what we know of the world has emerged, and with it a new kind of knowledge. It will also presuppose that there are disciplines which do not operate in this way and thus yield us something other than scientific knowledge. This may seem an elementary point, but it is crucial, and it is not without its critics.

Popper (1959) proposed a demarcation criterion between scientific and non-scientific hypothesis which centres on the notion of falsifiability: there must be states of affairs which are ruled out as impossible by a theory (shown to be logically incompatible with it), such that, if we were able to show that they held, we could show the theory to be falsified. If one imagines a theory from which no such state of affairs were deducible, then it is clear that it excludes nothing and will be true, no matter what; the content of such a theory is at best hard to establish. The content of a theory is therefore, for Popper, a function of its falsifiability: the more potentially falsifying states of affairs we can deduce from a theory, the greater its content.

Thus science proceeds, according to Popper, not by means of the accretion of a body of proved, and thus certain, facts about the world, but via a hypothetico-deductive process: we come up with conjectures, or general hypotheses, deduce statements concerning specific states of affairs from them, and test these by attempting to show them to be false. Popper has

7

stressed that there is no mechanical or statable means of arriving at a theory or hypothesis (wild guesswork, imagination, modification of existing ideas, applications of those from other fields: any of these may play a part in the formulation of a theory), and that this fact is of no great consequence: what counts is whether falsifiable hypotheses can be derived from the theory.

The question arises whether a theory that is falsifiable, but which we have consistently failed to falsify, should be considered a true theory. Popper's view is that we cannot ever consider a theory to be true; rather, one takes falsifiable but unfalsified theories to be our present best guess at what the object of inquiry is like, but a conjecture which is still open to refutation. This reflects Popper's view that there is a logical asymmetry between truth and falsehood: our tests may falsify our general hypotheses but may never confirm them. But theories which stand up well to batteries of attempts to refute them are thereby said by Popper to be *corroborated* (not verified): they are to be assumed to be valuable guesses at the nature of reality.

While Popper denies that we can speak of a true theory, there is a notion of *convergence upon the truth* in Popper's philosophy of science. That is, he allows that our theories may possess greater or lesser degrees of what he calls verisimilitude: through the process of falsification, we develop theories which come closer and closer to a true description of their object of inquiry, even though we can never claim that they are incontrovertibly true descriptions. The notion of truth is therefore present in Popper's philosophy, but its function is considerably weaker than it would be in a verificationist view of science.

Note that Popper's demarcation criterion is not a criterion of meaningfulness. Unlike the logical positivists (see 3.2), Popper has never proposed that non-scientific theories, theories which are unfalsifiable, are meaningless (it is clear how we could claim this, however: we would argue that the content of unfalsifiable theories is nil, that they are literally uninformative). Positivists of most persuasions have been anxious to show that science can be sharply distinguished from metaphysics, with the former, as opposed to the latter, based firmly on observation. But Popper's philosophy of science, though it includes a demarcation criterion, has always opposed this attempt to sever science and metaphysics, and has attempted instead to show what the relationship between the two is. He achieves this in two ways: (i) in his claim that all observation statements are theory-laden and (ii) in stressing the importance of 'metaphysical research programmes', the metaphors, myths, or broad pictures of the world upon which scientific theories are built.

To exemplify (i), take the setting up of a scientific experiment: in any experiment our theoretical assumptions will determine what will count as an observation; clearly, just any sense impression which occurs during an experiment will not necessarily be relevant. An itch in the experimenter's elbow during an experiment on loss of heat energy in a refrigeration system, for instance, or the colour of the room in which the experiment will take place might well be determined to be irrelevant to the experimental results. Nor are such things self-evidently irrelevant: we must *decide*, on the basis of our theoretical orientation, what is to be counted as being part of the result and what is not. If we are mistaken in this, we may not achieve the success we aimed for. An itch in the experimenter's elbow, or the colour of the room, just might turn out to be relevant to the result, and experiments have often taken place in which it turns out that some factor considered unimportant and not part of the evidence emerges as crucial for the experiment and the theory in question. In these cases, we have to revise our theoretical proposals and our interpretation of the evidence.

This is closely connected with (ii): our scientific theories are based on broad pictures of the way the world is; examples from the history of physical theory are the notion that the world is mechanistic, or consists of space inhabited by objects, or of space inhabited by forces. The importance of myths for Popper is that Western science has evolved, not by abandoning them, but by building upon them to the point of evolving falsifiable hypotheses from them.

Popper suggests that our perceptual system works in a way parallel to the way science works, with certain sense impressions being foregrounded and others relegated to the background in accordance both with our guesses or hypotheses as to what we are perceiving, and with the pictures or metaphors which can be very deeply embedded in our perceptual framework. The deeper a notion is embedded in our way of viewing the world around us, the more such notions appear 'directly observable'. The notion 'physical object', for instance, is thus deeply rooted in our way of viewing the world to such an extent that we take it as self-evident that physical objects exist. Notice that this is so even when changes in our scientific theories undermine the very notion 'physical object'.

Eddington (1927) makes a great deal of this in arguing for an idealist philosophy of science (see 3.3), pointing out that even with a notion as quotidian as 'table' we begin to see two quite distinct 'tables' emerging as realities as our theories develop: one which is solid and exemplifies our standard notion of everyday, medium-sized macrophysical object (of the sort whose existence in the 'real world' we are so certain), and another which consists largely of space inhabited by energies and forces. But we are justified in treating both of these 'tables' as inhabitants of the real world, and we need not resort to idealism to accommodate two such distinct interpretations of what sort of thing a table is. In this case, our every-day 'myth' of the physical object inhabiting space is built into our perception of the world, but could be shown to result from the underlying reality: solidity and liquidity can both be defined in terms of, and thus induced by, the movements of particles, even if our perceptual system does not allow us immediate access to them.

We may return to falsificationism at this point and ask whether it relies on or assumes an element of verificationism: surely we must take the observation statements (or basic statements,[1] in Popper's terminology), which falsify a hypothesis to be true, that is, to have been verified. Thus, if we have a theory which centres on the notion that our planet revolves around the sun (which, Popper points out, is a metaphor for talking about the world that may well have evolved from mythology), and if we deduce from this that solar eclipses will occur under certain specifiable conditions, then we must accept that our statements regarding eclipse phenomena are true. Popper has stressed (1982: vol, 1, p. 185) that we assume, but do not assert, the truth of such observation statements, and that we cannot do so, because of the nature of the relationship between observation and theory: observation statements are theory-dependent, and our theories are fallible. But, if we decide to accept a set of observation statements as true, then they will be logically compatible with some theories but not with others, and thus may falsify our theories. They may not, however, verify them.

A further query arises in connection with the sketch I have so far given of falsificationism: is it really the case that science proceeds in this way, with theories being abandoned or modified in the face of conflicting evidence? We will often, surely, hold on to a theory even in the presence of counter-evidence. It is quite clear that this is indeed the case, and it is as well now emphatically to challenge the popularly held, but quite mistaken, view that Popper has somehow been guilty of defending a naive 'instant falsificationism', according to which falsification is achieved via simple refutation by conflicting evidence, and the theory in question is immediately thereafter abandoned or modified. Popper has never claimed this; indeed, it is incompatible with his (1959) philosophy of science: if falsifying evidence comes in the form of basic statements, and those basic statements are fallible, since theory-impregnated, then counter-evidence is fallible.

Thus, whoever the proponents of the 'simplistic Popperianism' to which Pateman (1987:25) refers may be, they have never included Popper. It can be shown that Pateman is mistaken in claiming that Kuhn (1962), Laudan (1977), and Lakatos (1970) undermine Popper's falsificationism. Thus, we find in Popper (1959) the statement that 'no conclusive disproof of a theory can ever be produced', and yet, surprisingly, it continues to be supposed (as in Newton-Smith 1982: 72–6) that Popper represents a naive, instant falsificationism. Lakatos (1978) suggested that, given an inconsistent set of scientific statements (that is a set in which there is some sort of clash or contradiction between the members of the set), one must select from among them the following: (i) a theory under test and then (ii) an accepted 'basic statement', leaving the rest of the set of statements to serve as background knowledge against which a test will occur (these are the interconnected theoretical assumptions which are present as an integral part of the context in which a single hypothesis is tested).

Lakatos therefore suggests a version of falsificationism which allows for the following role for falsification: we allow that any part of the entire body of knowledge be amended in the light of a clash or inconsistency, such that the apparently falsified theory may be allowed to stand, even in the face of the conflicting basic statement. What this means is that we do not take falsification to be final and incontrovertible. This, however, has always been allowed by Popper, and Lakatos' work should therefore be viewed as a detailed, and valuable, historical investigation into the way in which falsification works, rather than a radical revision or undermining of the falsificationist view of science.

Since Popper was never guilty of instant falsificationism, it could not have been improved upon by Kuhn (1962), and Popper (1983) may be right in suspecting that it was Kuhn himself who originated and perpetuated the 'naive falsificationist' Popper as a straw man for the benefit of his own methodological writings. For Popper's setting straight of the record on falsificationism, see his 1982 introduction to the (1983: xxxi–xxxv) *Postscript to the Logic of Scientific Discovery*. It should be noted, though, that Popper is not quite fair to Lakatos in the *Postscript*, since Lakatos does go some way towards debunking the myth of Popper the instant falsificationist by labelling him 'Popper0' and asserting that he never existed. As for Laudan (1977), his claim that, unlike his purportedly novel view of scientific progress, 'no major contemporary philosophy of science allows for conceptual problems' (p. 66) is patently false and his central notion, that science is essentially a problem-solving activity, far from constituting a new model of the growth of scientific knowledge, is entirely Popperian.

The crucial point for Popper's demarcation criterion is that a theory must be falsifiable *in principle*, where this is a purely logical matter; its history thereafter is not a simple affair, and will involve crucial decisions not only about what counts as counter-evidence, but also about the point at which a theory is in serious trouble. And at all of these stages the fallibilism which constitutes the core of Popper's methodology prevails. As Popper (1983:xxii) correctly states, there has been a widespread failure in the literature on falsificationism to recognise the crucial distinction between the falsifiability in principle of a hypothesis and the matter of whether and how we choose to abandon a theory in the face of falsifying evidence; it is precisely this failure which vitiates Newton-Smith's (1981) objections to Popper's falsificationism. Falsifiability is not established by demanding of scientists that they specify the conditions under which they would be willing to abandon their theory or hypothesis; it is a logical property of hypotheses, and is established by demanding to know what propositions (describing states of affairs) are logically incompatible with a given hypothesis.

Having established the fundamentals of Popper's fallibilism and falsificationism, it is interesting to consider the bearing they have on the matter of ostension. Harré (1972:90–1), in his discussion of realism, proposes that we can provide the final incontrovertible proof of the existence of something by successfully demonstrating it, having referred to it. However, if the act of demonstration does depend on our theoretical apparatus, and if that apparatus is at all subject to revision, then so are our acts of demonstration. Now, since it is evident that our theories are thus subject to revision, it is clear that our acts of demonstration are too. And, if we consider whether our theories are capable of being said to be incontrovertibly true, we can decide whether the act of demonstration provides us with the incontrovertible evidence of the existence of an entity that Harré says it does.

Take a simple case of ostension: we point to an object and accompany our pointing with an utterance of the sentence: 'This is a fish.' On the face of it, we are dealing with a simple observation statement which is pretty well free of metaphysical import; the statement is plainly true or false depending on the state of affairs obtaining at the time and place of utterance. But, in pointing at, say, a whale, our assumption as to the truth or falsity of the statement has clearly changed over time, and this results from the fact that observation terms such as 'whale' and 'fish' are embedded in and derive their meaning from our theories of the natural world. What appeared to be demonstrably a fish at one stage in the development of our theories turned out to be demonstrably not a fish at a later stage. We can see from this that it would be perverse to suggest that we should not build a rather large amount of fallibilism into our view of scientific theories, given that they so frequently change. And, with this in mind, it would be absurd to assume that any given theory is not subject to revision, often radical revision to the point where the theory is abandoned altogether.

Harré (1972: 160–3) does not in the end allow that the meaning of terms can be fixed by ostension or that a given term can ever have any permanently fixed epistemological status. He allows, like Popper, that we cannot gain any knowledge of our world without the aid of theoretical devices, but this observation is in conflict with the idea that demonstration provides us with incontrovertible proof of existence. However, he does want to maintain an interesting dichotomy between two sorts of term, one of which would seem to provide some support for the idea of proof of existence via demonstration. His first sort is exemplified by the construct 'force' in physical (specifically, mechanical) theory: it can, he maintains, be eliminated from mechanics without major change to the theory. Thus, in analyses relying on the equation $F = ma$, any statement containing the expression 'force' could be translated into an equivalent one without the expression. The function of the construct 'force' is therefore, Harré implies, largely pragmatic: it allows us a useful amount of economy of expression. He contrasts this with expressions like 'virus', which cannot be thus eliminated without abandoning the theory of the virus altogether. The virus construct also seems to gain from the fact that we can reasonably speak of seeing viruses whereas we cannot in principle speak of observing forces.

But this dichotomy can be elucidated by means of Popper's philosophy of science: while we want to say that there really are such things as viruses in the world, and that they existed before we discovered them (these are indeed realist assumptions), we are forced to accept that, as with whales, the most we can be certain of is that there is something there when we point it out. As to what its description might be, and as to whether two objects count as instances of the same thing, only our theories and the requirements we make of them can tell us. Forces are no more or less pragmatic in their function than constructs relating to objects such as viruses. And, while the general notion 'force' differs from the 'virus' construct in that it can be viewed as a metaphor underlying our theories, a part of the metaphysical research programme which takes the world to consist of space inhibited by forces, we can derive from this metaphor hypotheses concerning specific sorts of force which can be tested.

I should answer a couple of possible objections to Popper's proposals at this point. One of them is that Popper, in emphasising the theory-dependence of observation, might be said to be denying the possibility that there is a theory-external world to be described by our theories. Popper's position is that we make the *assumption* that there is indeed a theory-external world, and this is mirrored in his adoption of a correspondence theory of truth (see Popper 1959:274). He stresses that the claim that there is a theory-external world is a metaphysical one (as is the claim to the contrary), and that such metaphysical positions are an unavoidable part of the process of constructing and evaluating scientific theories.

Another objection to Popper's realism is this: that there is surely some kind of continuity between the earlier and later meanings of terms in our theories. That is, to return to the 'fish' example, there are surely certain core semantic notions which link our earlier and later conceptions of what is to count as a fish. What has happened is that we have simply refined our definition of 'fish': the fundamental meaning remains the same from original to successor theory. An even stronger version of this objection would claim that it is the essential definition that remains unchanged, and that to define an entity is to isolate its essential properties.

This second objection is an interesting one. It certainly seems as if much of the original definition of 'fish' (which included whales) is unchanged in its current meaning. This is an entirely *post hoc* assumption, however. There is no way of knowing in advance which aspects of our theories will change, and it is only from the perspective of the later theory and its terms that we establish what we take the essential or central components of those terms to be. Thus essentialist realism, or essentialism (Popper 1963: 97–120), the view that we arrive at a definition of the essence of an entity via our theories, does not reflect the provisional nature of theory construction and refutation. With the adoption of Popper's version of realism, we move away from the idea that we can incontrovertibly establish what the properties of the external world are.

This relates to the fact that single terms do not change their meaning independently of the entire conceptual system within which they are located: as the entire network of theoretical assumptions changes, so do the single terms embedded within them, and, since we cannot tell just how our theories will change, so we cannot tell which aspects of the meaning of a term will count as the central ones and which will not. This point bears very closely on the question of falsification: it is arguable that single hypotheses alone are not susceptible to disconfirmation (see 1.2 for discussion of this argument, often referred to as the Duhem–Quine thesis), since a given hypothesis and the terms contained in it gain their meaning from an entire network of theoretical assumptions.[2] This means that, in attempting to falsify a single hypothesis, we attempt to falsify the set of assumptions underlying it. In my example, it means that our definitions of 'fish' and 'mammal', and much of our theoretical apparatus concerning the natural world, are subject to revision, and that incontrovertible proof of existence is therefore not available to us.

But a rather serious problem remains: if we are not justified in allowing that there is some kind of semantic continuity from a theory to its successors, are we not then committed to denying that successive theories are talking about the same thing? Are we not then forced to say, with Feyerabend (1975), that they are incommensurable, that their terms have entirely different sets of referents? Well, we would be if we did indeed claim that there is no semantic continuity, but we need not make this claim; what must be denied is that we can isolate in advance what the semantic continuity will be. Putnam (1962) makes an interesting comment on this matter: he notes that any statement of even the most observational sort will necessarily contain terms which are informal in nature, and not quite explicitly defined. This suggests something like referential 'open-endedness' for our theoretical terms, and also supports the notion that ostension is probably not the *sine qua non* for the act of reference that Harré supposes it to be. Thus, with a 'principle of charity' (Putnam 1982; for discussion, see 1.2), we can take it that there are shared referents across successor theories.

Boyd (1979) also makes an important observation on the nature of reference in science. It concerns what he refers to as 'theory-constitutive' metaphors and the 'implicit' reference that they allow us:

There exists an important class of metaphors which play an important role in the development and articulation of theories in science ... They are used to introduce theoretical terminology where none previously existed ... their success depends on their 'open-endedness', i.e. they do not convey quite specific respects of similarity and analogy ... Theory-constitutive metaphors, when they refer, refer implicitly, in the sense that they do not correspond to explicit definitions of their referents, but instead indicate a research direction toward them. The same thing is apparently true of theoretical terms in science generally. (Boyd 1979:363)

Boyd claims that this use of metaphor is a device for 'accommodating our linguistic categories to the causal structure of the world so that they "cut the world at its joints"' (1979:358). Thus the reference of a general term is very much a matter of the 'epistemic access' it allows us to a particular sort of natural phenomenon. It would seem that the construct 'virus' is very much of the theory-constitutive sort.

Under such a realism, we can allow that there is no such thing as final, incontrovertible proof without abandoning the central realist notion that there is an extra-theoretical world which our theories are designed to describe. We also allow that ostension and the act of reference are very much theory-dependent, and, if we allow that our theories are subject to radical revision, then we allow that the acts of ostension and reference are too. But, if we take it that it is the properties of a theory-external world that induce the results of our tests, then we can maintain the realist idea that we are attempting to describe the properties of a world outside of our theories.

There are several elements in this version of a falsificationist realism that might appear to undermine the very basis of realism. The non-realist might respond, for instance, by claiming that, in allowing for the heavily theory-dependent nature of falsification, we are close to abandoning the idea that scientific theories are potential descriptions of reality. And, in abandoning this, we abandon the very core of realism, since it is precisely this claim that the instrumentalist objects to. It should be clear from this that scientific realism is open to many objections, to which I now turn.

1.2   The instrumentalist case against realism

A great many of the instrumentalist objections to realist interpretations of theories centre on the relationship between 'observation' and theory. It is felt by instrumentalists of most persuasions that science is best characterised as an activity that values observability ('the observable facts') highly, and this is probably a view that would gain widespread 'common-sense' support. On the face of it, this certainly seems to be a fair attempt at saying what science is all about. The dissatisfaction that many instrumentalists feel with theoretical constructs concerns the distinction between these and the observable facts. Scientific knowledge does, in some serious sense, consist in the steady accretion of known facts, and it is getting the facts right that counts; theoretical constructs are therefore best viewed as no more than our means of achieving this. Any attempt to elevate theoretical constructs such that we claim that they refer to extra-theoretical entities over and above the observable facts is regarded as overstepping the mark, and, in particular, any metaphysical content in scientific theories is regarded with suspicion.

These sorts of notion underlie, in the late nineteenth century, the work of Mach, in early twentieth-century philosophy of science, that of Duhem and Poincaré and, in the 1930s, logical positivism. Nor have such views on the nature of scientific theories ceased since the demise of logical positivism; the anti-realist lobby is as strong today as ever (see van Fraassen's 1980 'constructive empiricism' and the Dummettian anti-realist lobby in the theory of language reported in Luntley 1982).

As one might expect, this emphasis on observation rather than theory is often accompanied by an attempt to provide a strict delimitation between observation language and theoretical language (this is especially so of logical positivism). However, since I have argued in the previous section that such a delimitation is difficult to make, precisely because it is methodologically ill-conceived, I will concentrate here on what I take to be the strongest aspects of the instrumentalist challenge to realism, rather than on the observation/theory division, which is probably one of the weakest points in the range of instrumentalist proposals. We will, however, return to the observation/theory dichotomy in the discussion of logical positivism and its relation to instrumentalism in linguistics (in 3.2).

In order to get at the heart of this debate, it is necessary to unpack the notion 'instrumentalism', and examine the cluster of issues that have divided realists and instrumentalists. Once this is done, it becomes less important whether a given philosopher is regarded as belonging to one camp rather than another. Rather, what does matter is where different philosophers stand on the various issues. (Thus such questions as to whether Duhem was 'really' a realist are seen to be less important than where Duhem stands on the core issues.) Following Worral (1982), I consider them under two main headings: 'transcendence of data by theory' and 'overthrow of theories'; under each heading, several distinct but related issues are presented and discussed in relation to realism.

Transcendence of data by theory

One point made about the relationship between theories and 'the facts' is as follows: for any given empirical domain, there will be more than one possible theory consonant with the facts. This should suggest to us that we ought to be rather wary about the claims we make for the constructs in a given theory (such as interpreting them as descriptions of an underlying reality behind the phenomena). Consider the following statements by Duhem:

> When these hypotheses have enabled us to decompose the complex movements of the planets into simpler ones, we should not think that we have now come upon the real movements that lie behind the apparent ones. The real movements are the apparent ones. The end achieved is more modest: we have simply made the celestial phenomena accessible to calculation. (1969:20)

> Since the astronomer's hypotheses are not realities but merely fictions, the whole purpose of which is to save appearances, we should not be surprised that different astronomers attempt to achieve this purpose by means of different hypotheses. (p. 22)

> the hypotheses of physics are mere mathematical contrivances for the purpose of saving the phenomena. (p. 112)

That is, the fact that theories transcend the data, or, put another way, that theories are underdetermined by the data, is taken as a reason for making fairly modest claims about the status of theoretical constructs. Quine is frequently cited in this respect too; according to his 1953 work, our theoretical constructs (including those referring to physical objects) are to be taken as 'myths': 'viewed from within the phenomenalist conceptual scheme, the ontologies of physical objects and mathematical objects are myths. The quality of myth, however, is relative; relative, in this case, to the epistemological point of view. This point of view is one among various, corresponding to one among our various interests and purposes' (1953:19).

There are several related views connected with this. One is the pragmatist position that our theories are best evaluated in relation to our purposes rather than in relation to their correspondence, or degree of correspondence, to an extra-theoretical reality. This pragmatic strand is common among instrumentalists, and can be easily detected in the above quotations from Duhem and Quine. It is explicitly spelled out in the following statement by Quine: 'Our standard for appraising basic changes of conceptual scheme must be, not of a realistic standard of correspondence to reality, but a pragmatic standard' (1953:79).

The two notions, theories as myths, and evaluation of theories in purely pragmatic terms, are frequently linked, thus: 'the myth of physical objects is epistemologically superior to most in that it has proved more efficacious than other myths as a device for working a manageable structure into the flux of experience' (Quine 1953:44).

Because theories are thus underdetermined by data, it is possible, for any given theory, to construct an alternative, logically distinct theory which entails the same body of data. This is often referred to as the underdetermination thesis, and is closely linked with the Duhem–Quine thesis, which can be stated thus: any theory can be protected from falsification, when faced with contradicting evidence, by means of adjustments to some part (or parts) of the theory, or to the background knowledge within which it is located.

One of Quine's points in this respect is that single hypotheses themselves are not susceptible to disconfirmation, but only theories as wholes; thus a single consequence of a theory, when in conflict with experience, can be saved by adjustments to the theory. Quine (1953 and elsewhere) also distinguishes between experiences which are on the 'periphery' of our theoretical scheme of things and those closer to the centre, so that ordinary everyday macrophysical objects such as 'table' are apparently observable, owing to their being instances of 'physical object', a notion so central to our conceptual scheme as not to appear theoretical at all. Note that this way of dealing with the difference between observation language and theory language is distinct from the logical positivist attempt (as in Carnap's 1937 *Logical Syntax*) to distinguish sharply between observation and theory. The principal problem with it is that, while it does allow that even terms like 'table' are theoretical, i.e. are part of our conceptual scheme, it creates a very vague scale of theoreticity, where it is not clear how we go about determining the degree to which a term is theoretical. It is similar in this respect to Lakatos's distinction between the 'hard core' and the 'protective belt' of theories.

How should the realist respond to these points, and to what extent do they seriously undermine realism? Regarding the interpretation of theories as myths, it need not concern the fallibilist realist that this is so. Under

Popper's version of realism, many of our scientific theories do in fact start out as myths, but the important distinction between non-scientific myths and scientific theories is that the latter are testable (i.e. falsifiable); Popper is quite happy to allow that our scientific theories are embedded in 'metaphysical research programmes' which are a kind of general picture of the world.[3]

Of course, Quine allows that our scientific 'myths' are epistemically superior in this way, but does not stress that, in thus being superior, they allow us something new, namely access to the world, knowledge of it, and progress in developing that knowledge.

The crucial point here is that at which the realist decides that it is more likely that there are physical objects in the world than it is that there are Homeric gods, but, for Quine, this is going too far: all we are warranted in claiming is that the former is an epistemically superior myth, and therefore to be believed in more readily than the latter. It is heuristic fruitfulness, when a given construct really does allow us progress, which is the major factor in favour of realism; of course, the instrumentalist takes just this fertility to be one of his major criteria for assessing theories. However, the realist can respond that it is hardly likely to be mere chance that one particular construct, or set of constructs, is more fertile than another. For the instrumentalist, there is nothing to be said about *why* one myth is superior to another, whereas the realist gives an account of the success of particular constructs: they are fair approximations of how the world is organised.

Regarding the pragmatic means of assessing theories, this is at best trivially valid, at worst inaccurate. Quine's claim that we should appraise changes in theoretical framework from a pragmatic standpoint *rather than* from a standard of correspondence to reality becomes empty if our pragmatic goal, our purpose, is to approximate, through our theories, the structure of the world; that is, if it is a realist purpose (and often it is). Duhem's response to this was that, even if our successful theories *are* constructed because of a realist attempt to describe the world, we should not confuse the motivation for a theory with its degree of success. In Duhem's words, we must distinguish between 'the chimerical hopes that have incited admirable discoveries' and the notion that such discoveries 'embody the chimeras that gave birth to them' (1953:32). However, this again undervalues *heuristic* factors: if a realist approach gives rise to progress, this suggests that it is the right approach, just as a given cluster of theoretical constructs which gives rise to success should be viewed as being on the right lines. Duhem's attempt to weaken the heuristic value of a realist approach can be encountered by the question: 'What *can* we do to validate a particular metatheoretical approach if not point to its success in research and discovery?'

It should also be noted that pragmatism of this sort easily leads to relativistic excesses of the sort in which there is nothing to choose between one way of describing the world and another, and where differences in conceptual scheme are simply reflections of different cultural outlooks (see Feyerabend 1975 for arguments against the rationality of science, i.e. in favour of the notion that scientific theories succeed by means other than the rational). Kuhn (1962) is rather guilty of this too;[4] the principal objection to it (Popper's) is that it denies the objectivity of science by viewing it as little more than a manifestation of social, personal, and political outlook. But the difference between our current view of the world and that which incorporates Homeric gods is not just a matter of different cultures choosing different conceptual schemes: our framework has allowed us knowledge and, more importantly, progress in a way which the panoply of Homeric gods could never have done; we are justified in claiming that we know more about our world via our scientific theories than was, or could be, known via the postulating of Homeric deities.

If 'theories as myths' and pragmatism are not worrying threats for the realist, the underdetermination thesis is often taken to be so. It has led realists such as Boyd (1973) to deny the possibility of underdetermination, and Worrall (1982), in accepting its possibility, to retreat to a very minimal realist position. It has induced Newton-Smith (1978) to adopt a position which he says is not realist in any currently understood sense, since, in his view, the possibility of underdetermination seriously undermines the realist position.

In discussing the underdetermination thesis, it is as well to follow Newton-Smith (1978) and distinguish between a weak and a strong interpretation. The strong interpretation (Quine's version) is that all theories are necessarily underdetermined by the data, such that, for any theory, there will always be an alternative, logically distinct theory which entails the same body of data. The weak interpretation states that theories can be but are not necessarily always so underdetermined. In addition to this, one can make more progress in assessing the threat posed by the underdetermination thesis if one distinguishes, along the lines suggested by Worrall (1982), between the general sense in which theory is underdetermined by data, and those cases where there does seem to be an insurmountable difficulty in choosing between alternative theoretical accounts of the same set of phenomena. The general sense in which theories are underdetermined by data is, as Worrall points out, a trivial consequence of the transcendent nature of our theories. We may take it to be a feature of our theories which supports realism, since it reverses the inductivist notion that observation is methodologically privileged with respect to theory.

Worrall also notes that, in describing two theories as equally warranted by the data, the instrumentalist must consider that mere 'alignment' with the data is insufficient to allow us to conclude that two theories are empirically equivalent: it is clear that considerations such as simplicity and unity or coherence internal to a theory will also guide us in judging one to be better warranted by the data than another (as both Duhem and Quine would allow). For the realist, it is the latter which is the best candidate as our present best guess.

Having said this, we have considerably reduced the range of cases where there could be said to be two logically distinct but empirically equivalent theories. However, there is a more worrying case, where there does seem to be a ready translation from one theory to a logically distinct alternative one which does seem to be worrying for the realist: in this circumstance, it would appear that either account of the world is possible, and that the realist must either illogically accept one to the exclusion of the other or abandon his realism.

As Worrall points out, there are two responses the realist can make to these points: one is that it is not normally the case that, with two extant theories of the same phenomena, there does exist a straightforward translation algorithm, and that the realist is therefore not normally faced with such a situation; another is that, in the cases where there really is such a direct translation, we simply do not have the means for deciding between the two rival theories, and that this situation in turn should be taken to indicate that we need to discover more, via development of existing theories, which would make ready translatability impossible and a choice possible. This suggests, again, that the realist position, as Feyerabend (1964) points out, is heuristically fertile in a way that the instrumentalist position is not: when faced with such a ready translatability, where there appears to be nothing to choose between two competing theories, the instrumentalist would simply accept the situation (this would appear to be Duhem's response, if one considers his comments above). The realist, however, finds it unacceptable, and this spurs him on to richer development of the theories in question, and the possibility of discovery resulting from this.

The underdetermination thesis, then, is not as worrying to the realist as it may seem, but the Duhem–Quine thesis is a major worry, for several reasons, the principal one being this: if a major component of instrumentalism is the claim that theories are neither true nor false, and if, as falsificationist realists, we have abandoned any simple verificationism whereby theories can be said to be indubitably true, then it is essential that falsification is possible, otherwise we end up accepting that our theories can be neither verified nor falsified. To accept this is to abandon realism altogether and allow that our theories are indeed neither true nor false.

The realist must therefore deal with one of the points on which Duhem and Quine express the same view: the possibility of falsifying single hypotheses. Both point out that a given prediction (upon which one might devise a crucial experiment) is usually based on several assumptions which either are internal to the theory or are part of the assumed background knowledge within which the theory is located (part of the 'metaphysical research programme', in Popper's terms). It is from a combination of these factors that consequences of the theory are deduced, and therefore any clash between the consequences so deduced and experimental results does not constitute a direct falsification of a single hypothesis but a problem for the theory and its background knowledge taken as a whole. Thus disconfirmation can be avoided by suitable adjustments to the theory and/or its background knowledge.

In order to assess the degree of difficulty created for the realist, it is important to distinguish between various versions of the Duhem–Quine thesis. A very strong interpretation, that which Quine appears to be making (though see the reservations expressed in his reply to Grünbaum, in Quine 1976) is that auxiliary devices are always available when such a clash between a theory and experimental results occurs. As Grünbaum notes, the onus is on the proponents of such an interpretation to provide a demonstration that, for any set of data deduced from a specific hypothesis (the 'target' hypothesis), there will be a set of non-trivial auxiliary hypotheses which, together with the 'target' hypothesis, will guarantee the same set of results. It is also necessary to stress the importance of the non-triviality requirement here: if all Quine is saying is that there will be some set of auxiliary hypotheses, no matter how *ad hoc* and inelegant, then this is rather a trivial remark and certainly not a matter of concern for the realist. Grünbaum points out that, because it cannot be guaranteed that such a saving set of hypotheses will exist in any given case, this strong version of the Duhem–Quine thesis is a logical *non sequitur*: from the occasional inconclusiveness of crucial experiments, Duhem assumes inconclusiveness to be the rule.

It seems clear that this strong version of the thesis is not especially interesting. Consider, however, the weaker claim that we may in fact find that an appropriate set of saving hypotheses is available in some cases, and that falsification becomes impossible under those circumstances, and, following from this, that we cannot ever be certain that such a set of devices is not available in any given case. This seems a valid enough point. However, I do not think that it entirely undermines the sort of falsificationist realism adopted by Popper, though it does force some sort of retreat from the strongest versions of falsificationism (the sort Lakatos 1970 refers to as 'naive', as distinct from his weaker 'sophisticated' version). Popper allows that single hypotheses are tied both to the internal structure of the theory and to the background data in the way indicated, and he also accepts that there is a strong conventionalist element in our background knowledge, which is assumed but not accepted as confirmed, or even probable. All of this is part of Popper's fallibilism, in which we cannot be sure of the foundations upon which our theoretical frameworks are built, but we can none the less get falsifiable theories out of this construction and thus make progress; furthermore, we may be able to pinpoint the part of a theoretical network which is responsible for the collision with experimental results.

The Duhem–Quine thesis does not, of course, amount to a claim that entire theories are unfalsifiable; rather it asserts that only whole theories, and not specific hypotheses, are falsifiable. Thus, falsification, even if only of entire theories, is still possible. Acceptance of this observation led Lakatos (1970) to stress that, even if we accept that 'instant' falsification of the sort assumed by the 'naive' falsificationist is rarely possible, falsification is indeed possible in terms of 'progressive' as opposed to 'degenerating' problem shifts, where the odds against a particular theory mount as attempts to save it not only become excessively *ad hoc* and inelegant, but also decline into lower and lower degrees of empirical yield.

It may seem that, once we get to this stage, we are dealing with a very much modified version of falsificationist realism, but it is important to bear in mind Popper's distinction between the purely logical matter as to whether a hypothesis is falsifiable (whether there are states of affairs with which it is incompatible) and the matter of the stage at which we abandon the modification of a theory in the face of conflicting evidence. It is this latter issue which Lakatos is addressing. The strictly logical issue of falsifiability of hypotheses is distinct from that of the way in which theories are eventually abandoned, even if the one has implications for the other. And, while a single hypothesis does indeed depend for its meaning upon a host of auxiliary hypotheses, this reflects the fundamental revisability of our theories, which is fundamental to Popperian realism.

Realism, then, is able to survive the set of instrumentalist challenges connected with the notion of transcendence of data by theory; however, these do not exhaust the range of possible serious objections to realism, the remainder of which are grouped together here under the heading 'overthrow of theories'. As will become apparent, both the under-determination thesis and the Duhem–Quine thesis re-emerge as being equally problematical when one comes to consider the development of theories and the manner in which one theoretical framework gives way to another.

Overthrow of theories

Major discontinuities in scientific theories seem to lend credence to the instrumentalist claim that theories come and go, but that what matters is that there is a steady build-up of empirical results which constitutes real progress. Attached to this is the notion that the real descriptive part of a superseded theory lives on when old theories are replaced. The instru-mentalist can claim that the realist is faced with insurmountable difficul-ties in trying to show that there is either (a) semantic continuity from one theory to its successor or (b) any sort of convergence or approximation towards the truth, in the sense of Popper's verisimilitude. If the instrumen-talist is right about this, then it does look as though we have either discrete changes from one theoretical framework to another, and only a build-up in the range of phenomena dealt with constituting progress, or old theor-ies changing like shifting networks, almost independently of the data. Either way, our theories begin to look like dispensable instruments for achieving greater degrees of empirical success.

Both the Duhem–Quine thesis and the underdetermination thesis lend weight to this challenge: the idea that we can accommodate recalcitrant experiences by means of adjustments to the system supports the general picture of our theories as shifting networks which are only tenuously con-nected to the phenomena we want them to account for, and this picture of theory development strengthens the notion that they should be treated as dispensable instruments. The underdetermination thesis would lead us to expect radical discontinuities as the norm: they would follow from the fact that it is always possible to construct a logically distinct alternative theory for any given range of phenomena.

Regarding the notion that the semantic core of a theory is transmitted to successor theories, we saw in the previous section that we could only be certain that some part of the meaning of theoretical terms would be thus transmitted, but not which part or how much. The trouble is that it is only once we actually have the successor theory that we can outline the aspects of the meaning of its terms which are shared with its predecessor. It would be impossible to predict in advance what the shared elements might be. Thus, for example, what seems to the Einsteinians to be the core of Newtonian mechanics is unlikely to have appeared thus to the Newtonians.

This seems to lend credence to Feyerabend's (1975) notion of the 'incommensurability' of theories: semantic continuity from a given theory to its superseding theory is impossible, and thus a term like 'electron' in one theory of the structure of the atom has neither the same sense nor the same denotation as the same term in the later theory. This objection can be rebuffed, however. Recall (1.1) Putman's (1960) notion of referential open-endedness, according to which fundamental terms are not fully defined. This notion can be combined with his (1975, 1982) response to the problem of continuity, in which he appeals to what he calls the principle of charity (or principle of the benefit of the doubt): scientific terms are not synonymous with descriptions; a term such as Bohr's 'electron' may thus have a different description from our current term of the same name, but the two are 'approximately' about the same thing, in virtue of their referential open-endedness. Thus, both Bohr's term and ours may be used to refer.

However, one must then beware of claiming that any theoretical construct, once postulated, can be used to refer successfully to an extra-theoretical entity. We must allow that some terms are abandoned because their function in theories causes complexity and failure to account elegantly for the phenomena, and this is as good a reason as any for saying that they cannot be used to identify objects of reference. How then does the realist account for terms like 'phlogiston', which entity, he claims, has never existed? Putnam's proposal is that, for the principle of the benefit of the doubt to operate, other factors must be in place, such as our capacity to account for the same range of phenomena dealt with under the previous theory. Since such factors were not in place when phlogiston theory was superseded, and the account given of the phenomena by 'phlogiston' did not live on as a limiting case in the subsequent theory, we can conclude that the term did not then and does not now count as an object of reference. In this account, heuristic and methodological criteria for decisions about the status of our constructs are stressed, and this does seem to be a reasonable way of assessing such cases.

These considerations bear directly on the second of the two problems in question, the difficulty the realist has in maintaining that science is convergent upon the truth, that we achieve progress by means of greater and greater degrees of approximation to the truth via the process of falsification (Popper's notion of verisimilitude and its concomitant notion, 'corroboration'). If we do face this difficulty in maintaining that there is some sort of semantic continuity between successive theories, how can we sustain the idea that our theories gradually allow us to build up an increasingly faithful picture of how the world is? The most extreme response that I know of to this is Worrall's (1982), in which he abandons verisimilitude altogether and concedes that our superseded theories are not approximately true, but plain false. This leaves him with an absolutely minimal version of realism: we cannot know that our theories are true, nor can we claim that they approximate a correct account of the structure of the world via the process of falsification.

We need not go as far as Worrall does in responding to the problem of convergence, however. We can make a fair amount of headway in retaining convergent realism if we adopt something like Boyd's (1973) version of approximation to the truth, which runs along the following lines. Boyd makes the (rather extreme) claim that realism should be taken to be an *empirical hypothesis*, and, furthermore, one which is true, and which has explanatory force in accounting for why scientists (who, he says, are realists by virtue of their practice) behave as they do and why science succeeds. Thus, the idea that science approximates an objective truth is seen as an empirical hypothesis supported by the facts of scientific practice.[5] There is indeed something explanatory in the realist position in that it does allow us to give an account of why our theories succeed, though, unlike Boyd, we need only take this to be a factor in favour of realism as a methodological stance rather than as an empirical hypothesis. However, the point remains that, if we can maintain a version of a theory of correspondence between our theories and the world, and if we suggest that it is some kind of approximation to the structure of the world that allows our theories to succeed, then the notion of verisimilitude is salvageable, and with it semantic continuity.

There is one further point against instrumentalism which must be made, relating to idealisation. It has been taken by some (e.g. Duhem) to be an argument for instrumentalism that our theories possess a precision that is not mirrored in the phenomena they account for, and that we must therefore see them as idealised fictions which are not to be confused with the real observable data. This is probably, along with the proposed distinction between observation and theory language, one of the weakest instrumentalist claims; it is easily turned to the realist's advantage: not only are our theories thus idealised, but they must be. It is not clear that we could gain any knowledge of our world otherwise, and, if idealisation allows us progress in the way it does, this can be taken to suggest rather strongly that our idealised theoretical constructs are indeed a fair guess at the structure of the world which includes the phenomena. Again, there is no way of accounting for the success of our theories other than by adopting this realist position, the principal warrant for which is heuristic fertility.

Itkonen's (1983:129) objection to this, that there is no non-circular definition of success, that the success of an activity depends on its purpose, and thus the criterion for success changes with changing purposes, is not something the realist need worry about. It reflects the sort of relativism that results from a philosophy of science, such as those proposed by Kuhn and Feyerabend, which overemphasises the social aspect of scientific activity. To reply to this, we need to start from the rather evident fact that Western science is more successful than African witchcraft; one need only establish what the witchcraft practitioner himself wants to count as success (let us say in the realm of physical healing or weather prediction) to see that Western science is usually more successful *on his terms* as well as on ours (why should Itkonen assume that these are so different anyway? It seems rather evident what any culture will want to count as success in the way of dealing with, say, healing and weather prediction). Note the pragmatist element in Itkonen's view, which can be accused of being trivially self-evident in the same way as Quine's is. It is clear that, if we take a position such as Itkonen's seriously, then the entirety of the framework of rational inquiry descends into a kind of relativism, which is precisely what Feyerabend (1975) proposes. But this social relativism is weak in that it centres on the trivially true claim that any framework will work better for us than none at all; that does nothing to impugn the fact that some frameworks are clearly better than others, and we require an account of why this should be so.

It should by now be clear that suitably sophisticated versions of instrumentalism and of realism end up being *almost* identical, since they both incorporate the central theme of stressing heuristic fertility. However, it seems to me that they are not identical, and that they may be separated by what could be called the realist's assumption, that it is the nature of reality which causes one theory to be more fertile than another. That a mere assumption divides the two in their more sophisticated forms may seem scant reason for taking them to be distinct, but it is an assumption which is of enormous importance, reflecting as it does the essentially scientific desire to know why some frameworks are more successful than others. It is this desire which results in the kind of progress which is the hallmark of scientific knowledge.

2 *A realist philosophy of linguistics*

2.1   Falsification and observation

Having considered the general issues connected with Popper's version of
realism and the instrumentalist objections to it, I turn now to the question
of how it applies to theory construction in linguistics. In particular, let us
ask how, if at all, it applies to theoretical linguistics, and in particular to
the generative enterprise.

We can begin with a few simple observations. It is a fact that there is
such an activity as theoretical linguistics. Whether it can be said to count
as a scientific enterprise is open to debate; I hope to show shortly that it is
clearly scientific. In most of its major journals, research is carried out
without recourse to quantification or statistical analysis. What is interesting is that this is possible: how can linguistic theories be proposed and
elaborated in the absence of experimentation, and independently of any
knowledge of cognitive psychology or social theory? What is the object of
inquiry that allows this to take place? That some linguists may emerge in
work involving quantification or the assembling of corpora has no bearing
on the validity of investigating the fact that linguistic theorising takes
place with an evidential basis which is something other than a collection of
observed events. Let us refer to this activity as autonomous linguistics
(AL), and ask how it proceeds.

We need to ask to what extent method in AL mirrors that of the natural
sciences; this is a question of the *extent* of the methodological unity
between the two, and not a simple one of deciding whether AL is or is not
a scientific activity, *tout court*. Applying Popper's demarcation criterion
means asking whether theories in AL, or rather specific hypotheses derivable from them, can be said to be falsifiable, and in what way. It seems to
me that a clear case can be made for saying that linguistic hypotheses in
AL are testable against data consisting of sets of well-formed and/or ill-
formed expressions, and may be falsified by them. Indeed, generative

work in AL has proceeded with such a method for some time now. Thus, phrase-marker representations may embody claims about, among other things, syntactic constituency; if we have tests for constituency, then we can bring them to bear in testing those claims. Naturally, the validity of the notion 'constituency', and of the tests which we take to indicate it, is open to question, and will always remain so, but this is true, as we have seen, of any theoretical construct in any science, and does nothing to undermine the claim that syntactic hypotheses are falsifiable.

That linguistic hypotheses are testable, against something other than the observation of spatiotemporal events is made clear if we consider the claim, for instance, that a test for constituency within the noun phrase in English (let us say the 'one' substitution test for the constituent intermediate between noun phrases (NPs) and their head nouns, as described in Radford 1988 and Burton-Roberts 1986) allows us systematically to pick out a certain type of constituent, then we may test a variety of hypotheses ranging from the particular (does a given string form such a constituent?) to the general (e.g. is there a systematic distinction between complements of nouns and modifiers of the intermediate category?). It is precisely because these hypotheses are falsifiable that they have content: in testing them we make progress in investigating NPs in English. And the evidence brought to bear in that testing does not consist of sets of observed events.

Now, in a generative grammar, in which we postulate rules to generate representations, and to map representations on to representations (or rules on to rules), the rules themselves are not propositions, as Itkonen (1978) points out. They are not therefore the sorts of thing that are directly testable; but the claims embodied in our analysis are testable, where an analysis consists of rules and representations taken together. Propositions such as constraints on rules and representations are also testable (it is perfectly clear what sorts of expression will count as violations of the subjacency condition, for instance). It is certainly the case that what will count as evidence for or against a claim will be determined by the framework within which those claims are made, but this is true in any scientific domain, as we saw in 1.1.

Since, in the generative enterprise, we take these analyses to characterise what it is we know in knowing the language, what it is that we possess which enables us to make the intuitive judgements we make, we may reasonably be said to be making falsifiable claims about the nature of linguistic objects (in syntactic theory, objects such as sentences and their subparts) and our knowledge of them (that which allows us to know what counts as a sentence of a given language). I come to this shortly (2.3), and to the question of what it might mean to say that the objects of this know-ledge are properly described as constituting speaker-external states of affairs (2.5).

This testing of analyses in a generative grammar is exemplified in a phonological theory which allows of a distinction between underlying and surface representations, and in which phonological rules map one on to the other. Here, we cannot interpret the rules directly as propositions; rather, it is the entire analysis which will embody the claims we are making. To take an example: a standard generative phonological (GP) analysis of nasality in French vowels may contain a rule of the form

$[-\text{cons}] \rightarrow [+\text{nas}]/\_\_\_ C \begin{Bmatrix} \# \\ C \end{Bmatrix}$ which allows us to map one sort of repres-

entation on to another, where the significance of these representations is determined by the framework in which they are placed. The claim em-bodied in such an analysis is therefore that, given representations of the sort on the left of the rule, we will invariably map these on to a distinct sort of representation and in doing so express a general claim about French. The claim embodied in the analysis is not therefore falsified (*pace* Hooper 1976) by the attestation of surface phonetic sequences of the sorts [ṼCC], since the analysis does not embody the claim that such surface se-quences are ill-formed. What *would* falsify the claims here would be a state of affairs where, given the framework we are working within, we are obliged to allow the rule to operate where we would not expect it to, or not to operate where we would. It is thus the entire analysis, comprising rules and representations, which embodies a falsifiable claim.

It is certainly the case that some *ad hoc* measure could be proposed to obviate situations where the wrong output is achieved and thus where the claim embodied in the analysis is falsified, and, in this case, this might in-volve the postulating of underlying vowels without independent support. But, even were we to allow for *ad hoc* adjustments, we must concede that the claim made is sufficiently explicit to allow us to see clearly what would count as falsifying evidence prior to making the *ad hoc* adjustment, and thus falsifiability is achieved even where *ad hoc* solutions are found. Unless this were the case, we would be unable to assert that a solution *was* indeed *ad hoc*.

We can see a further parallel between the methodology of AL and Popper's view of how natural science works if we consider the 'metaphysical research programme' notion. In AL, we find that theories are indeed derived from underlying metaphors which are in themselves untestable: the notion that 'a language is a set of sentences' is not a falsifiable claim, and thus not a scientific hypothesis, but is the metaphor upon which the generative enterprise is built. From it, we can evolve theories of grammars which generate these sets, and the specific hypotheses flowing from these theories may be falsified.

We have seen that it is testing, the possibility of falsification, which distinguishes scientific from non-scientific disciplines. We can further distinguish among the sciences by distinguishing different sorts of testing, by asking what sorts of evidence can lead to falsification in different activities. It is clear that the evidential basis for linguistic theories is quite distinct in nature from the basic statement used in physical theory: for most subparts of linguistic theory, descriptive statements typically do not relate to spatiotemporal events, but are instead reports of linguistic states of affairs gained via acts of intuitive judgement (to check this out, one need only take a look at the evidence brought to bear in work published in the major theoretical linguistics journals). Given that those states of affairs are linguistic expressions consisting of linguistic objects (sentences and their subparts) and the relationships holding between them, it becomes evident what a realist version of the generative enterprise will look like.

Theorists, taking the underlying metaphor or metaphysical research programme of a language as a set of sentences, devise theories which define 'sentence' for a given language, providing semantic, syntactic, and phonological subparts of those theories, and using sets of expressions as the data which test hypotheses derived from those theories. The linguist can be said to be attempting to describe the mechanisms in the underlying linguistic reality which allow us to characterise these expressions as well-formed. In doing so, the notion 'rule' counts as a central metaphor: while we cannot falsify the claim that languages are rule-governed, we can judge the heuristic fertility of the metaphor and falsify claims about particular rules. Thus, neither the notion that languages are sets of sentences nor the notion that there are rules of languages constitute falsifiable claims, but this fact does not mean that generative linguistics is not a scientific enterprise, since these notions correspond to the metaphysical research programmes of natural science and, as in natural science, falsifiable claims are derivable from them.

There is a complication within theoretical linguistics concerning testing, however: the sets of expressions which act as evidence are gained via acts of intuitive judgements for syntax and semantics, but are gained only partially by this method in phonology, where phonetic transcription allows us to make something more akin to Popperian basic statements. Thus, although there is an asymmetry in evidence type between syntax and semantics on the one hand and phonology on the other, it is partial (phonologists too use intuitive judgements to access sets of expressions in, for instance, metrical theory, or more generally wherever perceptibly distinct sets of expressions can be presented to native speakers for intuitive judgement). This raises several issues concerning the status of phonology in relation to phonetics, to which I return in 6.3.

Consider now the nature of testing in psycholinguistics: here we typically rely on experimentation and corpora; the data are typically of the basic statement sort, relating to spatiotemporal events. As Itkonen (1978) has noted, there are crucially important non-spatiotemporal aspects of such events (their intentional and linguistic aspects) and any psycholinguistic theory will be dependent on expressions and hypotheses from linguistic theory in that its hypotheses cannot be be framed without these. The evidential distinction between AL, in which intuitive judgements play a major part, and psycholinguistic theory, where they do not, is clear, and it is this distinction which allows us to maintain that they are distinct sorts of enterprise.

Sociolinguistics also differs in evidence type from AL: like psycholinguistics, its results are derived from spatiotemporal events (again, granting that they are not merely events of the sort investigated in physical theory: they come about via linguistic, social, cognitive and specifically intentional states of affairs). They are, like psycholinguistic results, and unlike evidence in AL, amenable to quantification and thus statistical interpretation.

It seems clear that, on the basis of our consideration of scientific method in chapter 1, AL may be said to be scientific; but its evidential basis makes it methodologically distinct from both sociolinguistics and psycholinguistics; it is this fact and its consequences which I pursue in the following sections.

2.2   Deductive method in a non-nomic domain

One of the consequences of the claim that the evidence in AL does not consist of observations of events is that we cannot expect law-like explanations in AL, since laws are propositions concerning events. The standard deductive–nomological (D–N) explanation which Popper (1972:349–52) cites as causal scientific explanation consists of a general law and certain initial conditions from which the explicandum follows as a conclusion. On testing the deduced consequences of a general statement, we take constant conjunction of certain events to constitute a law-like state of affairs; thus our explanation is a causal one: the mechanism which is expressed in our law-like statement causes the phenomena reported in the deducted statement. Such a schema is not available to AL. AL is a non-nomic domain: the generalisations we express in it are not correctly construed as laws governing events. Thus nomological explanations are not available in AL by definition; nor are predictions.

This is not to say, however, that the hypothetico-deductive method does not apply; we have seen that indeed it does. We may still devise generalisations as hypotheses, deduce consequences from them, and test these. That is, we will want, for any hypothesis in AL, to discover what its consequences are, as we would in natural sciences. If these are testable, they can be said to have content, and we can claim to have come up with explanations if our generalisations withstand the tests we make of the consequences which follow from them. Such explanations are not causal in the usual spatiotemporal sense; it would not be accurate to say that in making them we may claim to have isolated some aspect of the nature of linguistic reality without which the states of affairs we are trying to explain would not have come about. Rather, our explanations show what it is that *constitutes* a linguistic state of affairs.

AL is thus methodologically distinct from natural sciences in that its general statements are not propositions about events, and are thus not laws in any sense, but is parallel to natural sciences in that both falsification and the hypothetico-deductive method are available to it. Thus one of the major points of Lass (1980), that standard D–N explanations are not available in explaining language change, may be extended to AL, but not his claim that we cannot thereby claim scientific status for our theoretical activities: the explanations we propose are deductive, if not nomological, and are, crucially, falsifiable.

It is clear in what ways this view of AL could be countered: one alternative is the attempt to construe the evidential basis of AL as consisting of events (as in Sampson 1976); another is the attempt to expand our notion of what is meant by 'causal' and by 'law' (this avenue is explored and adopted by Itkonen 1983, Adamska-Sałaciak 1986, and Pateman 1987). I show below (2.6) why I think that the first of these cannot succeed. Concerning the second approach, it is not clear what content the notion 'law' is left with if the laws we formulate are not subject to disconfirmation, as I fear they are not if we allow that they may operate 'transfactually' such that a given law may be prevented from producing effects in certain cases. I discuss this in more detail in 5.2, however.

Now, given the methodological distinction between AL on the one hand and both sociolinguistics and psycholinguistics on the other, I want to suggest, following Itkonen (1978), that the reason they are thus distinct is that they have distinct objects of inquiry, that one is in a very real sense investigating different sorts of things in these different disciplines. This assumption is, furthermore, perfectly consonant with the sort of realism we have been discussing: it amounts to taking the methodological divide between the disciplines to be an *explanandum* and providing as *explanans* the realist assumption that the divide exists because the world is actually differentiated in this way.

To return to the scientific status of the generative enterprise: if we maintain, as the underlying metaphor, that languages are sets of sentences, and if our theoretical account of a language defines 'sentence' for that language, then, as realists, we want to claim that sentences (and thus all of their semantic, syntactic, and phonological subparts, and the relations among them) are linguistic realities. We will also want to claim that the grammars we devise to generate these languages, and thus the rules formulated in those grammars, characterise linguistic realities of which we possess knowledge; it is these which give rise to our sets of well-formed and ill-formed expressions.

What we allow for here, in distinguishing AL from sociolinguistics and psycholinguistics, is the tripartite distinction drawn by Itkonen (1978) between these two categories of discipline and physical theory, in which the evidence relates solely to spatiotemporal events, unmediated by intentional states. I have no doubt that the range of science types is wider than this, and that the picture becomes increasingly complex when we come to examine the nature of testing in, for instance , biological and medical science. Nor have I addressed the question of where social theory fits into this picture. My aim, however, is not to spell out an all-embracing picture of science types, but to establish the position of AL and related disciplines in relation to natural science. There is sufficient methodological similarity between Popper's notion of what counts as scientific activity and the activities of theoretical linguists to get a realist interpretation of AL, combined with an 'objectivist' ontology of linguistic objects off the ground, but there are a number of problems, both methodological and ontological, attendant on such a view. I will address some of these now, and try to spell out what is meant by 'objectivist'.

2.3   Objective knowledge

With a clear basis for claiming that method in theoretical linguistics adheres to the model of deductive method described by Popper, I now want to propose, following a suggestion by Lass (1976), that the sort of ontology required for linguistic objects is something rather close to Popper's (1972) category of objective knowledge.

Adopting Popper's (1972) view of emergent realities and applying it to linguistic objects mean taking rules and sentences, and thus languages, to be largely autonomous with respect to speaker-internal states of affairs, but interacting with them, in a way that parallels the notion of modularity within the language itself. Since this view of linguistic objects as essentially public, speaker-external realities is marked as novel in the current climate of opinion on these matters, I give a brief outline here of the nature of Popper's objectivist epistemology, followed by some observed properties of linguistic objects which suggest that this objectivism is the right ontology for the objects of linguistic theory.

In devising an account of the growth of scientific knowledge, Popper has proposed that we ought not to take scientific theories to be about psychological states of affairs, or to constitute such. That is, while some subjective, psychological process occurs, internal to the scientist, as a part of the formulating of a scientific theory, that is no reason to assume that the theory, *qua* theory, is a psychological entity. Rather, it is the objective content of the theory which is important, and this, Popper argues, is not psychological in nature, but intersubjective. If one considers, for example, the following properties of a theory, one need make no reference to the psychology of the scientist: its falsifiability, its internal consistency, its relationship to other theories, the relations between its subparts, its relationship to the problem situation it is designed to resolve, and the context in which it is proposed (the context would in fact include the problem situation and any competing theories designed to resolve that situation: the two are closely interconnected).

As an illustration of this, Popper (1972:170–80) considers the case of Galileo's heliocentric hypothesis in general, and his theory of the tides in particular. Taking the first of these, it is clear that, regardless of either Copernicus' or Galileo's psychological states, the heliocentric hypothesis was falsifiable. Whether Copernicus was aware of it or not, it was possible to deduce from this hypothesis that the inner planets of the solar system would show phases parallel to those seen on the moon. The most import- ant point about this is that it is a consequence of the theory that phases will be observable on the inner planets, and this relation 'consequence of' is a relation between theory, corollary, and object. And, while this is no doubt a complex relationship, it is not a psychological one. We do not invent this particular consequence, though we do invent the theory which leads to it; rather, we discover it, if we are fortunate and clever enough. A particular proposition which is derivable from a theory may, in fact, never be discovered; but this is not to say that it does not exist. And the fact that a consequence of a theory may exist without anyone's ever noticing it is taken by Popper to suggest that its existence does not depend on factors regarding the cognitive make-up of its creator.

While it is clear that internal processes and states enter into the growth of scientific knowledge, it is a mistake to confuse these with objectively existing properties of theories and objective problem situations. Popper demonstrates this by showing the non-psychological nature of Galileo's adoption of an untenable, and ultimately false, theory of the tides. The psychologistic interpretation of Galileo's position on the subject claims that some sort of psychological state internal to Galileo caused him to reject the notion of lunar influence upon the tides. Of the many psycho- logistic 'explanations' (jealousy, ambition, dogmatism, aggressiveness, etc.) for Galileo's rejection of this notion, one is the hypothesis that he was 'psychologically attracted' to the idea of a circular motion (rather than an elliptical one).

Against this, Popper (1972:174) argues that such speculations are super- fluous to an understanding of the relation between the theory and the problem situation; he points out that Galileo adopted a mechanical con- servation principle for rotary motions, and that this principle, rather than Galileo's inner state, ruled out the possibility of interplanetary influences, such as the influence of the moon upon the tides. Thus, not only does Popper's approach allow us a greater understanding of the problem, its intellectual context, and Galileo's response, but it also makes it clear that, even if Galileo *were* 'psychologically attracted' to the notion of a circular motion, this would be irrelevant to the problem, its theoretical context, and the validity of Galileo's theory.

This claim that it is a mistake to interpret scientific knowledge exclusively as a kind of psychological state is seen by Popper as countering a tradition in philosophy whereby 'knowledge' is interpreted solely in a subjective manner. In this tradition the term is taken to refer to, for example, states of mind such as certainty or strong belief (Musgrave 1969 gives a good survey of this tradition). Popper argues that these are quite distinct from objective contents of theories, which are independent of belief. As an illustration of this, he cites Newton's attitude to the theory of interplanetary influence: Newton found it very difficult to believe that the theory could be valid, and thus was possessed of nothing like certainty or strong belief; and yet he still saw that the evidence suggested that the theory was valid. From this, we see that the attitude or mental state of the proposer of a theory is quite distinct from the properties of the theory itself, which constitutes scientific knowledge.

Having thus argued for the autonomous existence of theories, their properties, and the problem situations they relate to, Popper argues that we ought to recognise the fact of interaction between such objective realities and our subjective internal states. He illustrates this (1972:109) with a quotation from Heyting concerning Brouwer's invention of the theory of the continuum: 'If recursive functions had been invented before, he [Brouwer] would perhaps not have formed the notion of a choice sequence which, I think, would have been unlucky' (Heyting 1962:195).

We can follow Popper in analysing this state of affairs, thus: the forming of the notion of a choice sequence is an internal, subjective process. It arises in response to an external, objectively existing problem situation. Part of that situation is the set of then extant theories, and Heyting is pointing out that, had this situation been different (had recursive functions been invented), then Brouwer's internal process of invention might not have occurred. The interaction we want to investigate takes place between the external problem situation and the inner mental processes necessary to the invention of the hypotheses, and also between the product of this invention and the problem situation, which is altered once our product becomes part of it and its resolution.

This strikes me as being appealing not only as a picture of the complexity of the process of the growth of scientific knowledge, but as a picture which stresses the objectivity of science; as such it has been criticised by relativists such as Kuhn (1962) and, from a physicalist viewpoint, Feyerabend (1964). While I do not go into these criticisms here, my responses to relativism and physicalism are given in 1.2 and 4.1 respectively.

The idea of interaction seems fruitful too: the notion that psychological states ('world two' objects) can be said to interact with objective products of cognitive activity (which are 'world three' in their ontological status) allows us to build up a clear picture of the complexity of scientific progress. The same can be said for the notion of interaction between the physical world ('world one') and our psychological states: Popper wants to say that our intellectual products may have an effect on, and be affected by, the physical world via psychological states. Thus, our theories may influence our physical environment in any manipulation of the physical world we carry out, such as the building of bridges, tools, or machines. In these cases, we can say that our theories are in fact embodied in the very stuff of the physical world: a machine is more than a collection of physical objects, its structure and function are embodiments of theoretical constructs.

Popper takes our theories to be emergent realities, resulting from the evolutionary process:

in a material universe something new can emerge. Dead matter seems to have more potentialities than merely to produce dead matter. In particular, it has produced minds – no doubt in slow stages – and in the end the human brain and the human mind. (Popper & Eccles 1977:11)

I suggest that the universe, or its evolution, is creative, and that the evolution of sentient animals with conscious experience has brought about something new. These experiences were first of a more rudimentary and later of a higher kind; and in the end that kind of consciousness of self and that kind of creativity emerged which, I suggest, we find in man.

With the emergence of man, the creativity of the universe has, I think, become obvious. For man has created a new objective world of the products of the human mind. (p.16)

It is important to bear in mind that this notion of emergence is closely linked with Popper's philosophy of physics, in particular his view of emergence and interaction in the physical world itself, and, along with these, the idea that the physical world is not a closed system. Popper illustrates this view thus:

in a universe in which there once existed (according to our present theories) no elements other than, say, hydrogen and helium, no theorist who knew the laws then operative and exemplified in this universe could have predicted all the properties of the heavier elements not yet emerged, or that they would emerge; or all the properties of even the simplest compound molecules such as water. (Popper & Eccles 1977:16)

Popper is thus taking the physical world itself to be 'open-ended', capable of evolving in ways that cannot be predicted. This is important, I believe, because it means that, if we adopt Popper's suggestions and try to apply them to linguistic objects, we adopt an ontology which rests on a clear conception of the nature of the physical world, a conception which is non-reductionistic and allows for the emergence of the new sorts of reality, with interaction among real objects of distinct ontological status. It is this which makes it so suitable as an ontological framework for interpreting linguistic phenomena.

Human language occupies a central position within Popper's framework: he has stressed the idea that the emergence of language must have been central to the emergence both of higher mental capacities and of other 'world three' objects such as scientific theories: 'One of the first products of the human mind is human language. In fact, I conjecture that it was the very first of these products, and that the human brain and the human mind evolved in interaction with language' (Popper & Eccles 1977: 11).

The emergence of language, with its descriptive and argumentative functions, is important for Popper, since, by means of the language faculty, we are able to begin to formulate the beginnings of what later became scientific theories. And Popper makes a great deal of these functions of language in the evolutionary process (see Popper 1972:120, for example).

The essence of Popper's proposals are summed up thus:

few things are as important as the awareness of the distinction between the two categories of problems: production problems on the one hand and problems connected with the structures produced themselves on the other. My second thesis is that we should realise that the second category of problems, those concerned with the products in themselves, is in almost every respect more important than the first category, the problems of production. My third thesis is that the problems of the second category are basic for understanding the production problems: contrary to first impressions, we can learn more about production problems by studying the products themselves than we can learn about the products by studying production behaviour. This third thesis can be described as an anti-behaviouristic and anti-psychologistic thesis. (Popper 1972:113–14)

The sorts of problem investigated by the theoretical linguist are rather well described as belonging to Popper's second category. While linguistic objects are clearly not products of the consciously created sort that theories are, they may reasonably be taken to be products of the evolutionary process which are speaker-external.

Consider some of the ways in which linguistic objects may be said to be objects of public, speaker-external knowledge. The lexicon of a language is taken in much current linguistic theorising (see Kiparsky 1982) to be a complex and highly organised part of the language. Given that, in the generative enterprise, we take knowledge of the grammar of a language to define what it is we know in knowing the language, it is clear that we want to claim that the lexicon of a language is a linguistic reality. But that reality is not clearly an object of *individual* knowledge; it is not clear what it would mean to claim that each of us, as members of a speech community, possesses the lexicon *per se*. That we each possess a mental lexicon is uncontroversial, but it is not clear that these internal representations are isomorphous with what we investigate as the lexicon of the language *per se*. Rather, the latter is more easily interpretable as a public object.

Clearly, this claim does not amount to observing that no individual knows all of the possible words of the language, since these are infinite in number. It does amount to claiming that the individual does not know all of the existing lexical morphemes of the language, and that this set of morphemes is definable only over sets which constitute members of communities. Thus the publicness of the lexicon of a language is something irreducible to states of affairs within individuals. The observation that lexical meaning is not something which resides in the individual serves to strengthen this point: in uttering a word, we cannot *choose*, as individuals, to mean anything other than what the work means publicly. Word meaning is a public state of affairs.

If lexical meaning is indeed reasonably described as a public, speaker-external state of affairs, something which holds for a community, and not for individuals, then sentence meaning too has this ontological status. Thus the rules for semantic interpretation are public, and so are rules in general. And, if linguistic rules are public, so are the objects which they define: sentences and their subparts. Thus the syntactic, phonological, and semantic rules may be said to enjoy the same intersubjective status. Under this ontological interpretation of the generative enterprise, we may say that a language, constituted by its rules, is a public object.

That linguistic objects are public is made clear when we consider the generative definition of a language as a set of sentences. A defining property of these sets is their infinitude; under a realist philosophy of science we are warranted in saying that the infinitude of languages is a linguistic reality. Finiteness, on the other hand, is a defining property of human beings and thus of their cognitive make-up. Thus, the infiniteness of languages cannot by definition be a property of human cognitive psychology, and a distinction between linguistic facts and cognitive psychological facts emerges.

To show that this is not an unreasonable claim to make, let us consider some linguistic phenomena which are more easily interpretable if it is correct. Consider recursion as a property of syntactic rules. There is no doubt that highly recursive structures may be characterised as well-formed in a given language, despite being difficult to decode when uttered. This fact leaves us with the problem of specifying why it is that the well-formedness of the following is assured despite its being very hard to decode:

The man who has knowledge of the fact that the Prime Minister knows of the whereabouts of the leader of the opposition's secretary's files is under arrest.

The ontology adopted here allows us to take the linguistic well-formedness vs. acceptability distinction and understand why it is that, if both the determinants of strictly linguistic well-formedness and the determinants of acceptability are speaker-internal, there is no restriction whatsoever on our being able to define such objects as both linguistic and well-formed. If both the fact of the linguistic well-formedness of such sentences and the fact of their acceptability are speaker-internal, cognitive facts, to do with our cognitive make-up, how can it be that our cognitive resources allow for such structures and cannot cope with them at the same time? Are these two facts simply such radically distinct sorts of cognitive fact that they are not describable under the same sorts of statement about cognition, or is the latter no sort of cognitive fact at all, but a fact about the *results* of cognition, a public, speaker-external fact? If we assume that such facts are indeed public and not facts about human cognitive capacity, we provide an explanation as to why the two sorts of fact may coexist: they are facts about distinct strata of reality.

Further such explanations become available to us once we begin to take seriously the ontological distinction between strictly linguistic objects as public realities, and states of affairs which are not strictly linguistic. In order consistently to uphold the sentence/utterance distinction, we need to assume that sentences are abstract objects which do not exist in a context; as Burton-Roberts (1985) has expressed it, they are not events and do not occur. We cannot attribute spatial location to them, and yet it is perfectly reasonable to say that they are linguistic realities whose properties we may investigate. The ontological status here attributed to sentences fits rather naturally with the idea of objective knowledge, with the notion that linguistic objects exist in a public space as intersubjective objects of mutual knowledge, and not as objects in physical space. Burton-Roberts shows that we cannot consistently uphold the sentence/utterance distinction and at the same time allow that sentences occur in context. We have a clear choice to make here: (i) concede the abstract, intersubjective ontology of sentences, (ii) abandon the sentence/utterance distinction, or (iii) reinterpret it such that we are no longer committed to the abstract nature of sentences. I try to show in 6.4 that option (ii) will result in considerable loss of generalising power, and Burton-Roberts shows that the attempts at (iii) have effectively resulted in (ii).

As a consequence of the public nature of rules, most sorts of ambiguity are viewed as public states of affairs: there can be no such thing as ambiguity solely *for an individual*. Preference strategies for interpreting ambiguous strings, of the sort discussed by Kimball (1973), on the other hand, reflect properties of the speaker-internal human speech parsing mechanism (HSPM). With the adopting of an objectivist framework, a picture of the ontological diversity of matters linguistic and cognitive emerges: the grammar which constitutes the language is a public object, whereas the HSPM is a part of human psychology. In investigating the interaction between the two, we are investigating the interaction between distinct sorts of reality, and this explains why distinct sorts of method are required at each level: the methods of cognitive psychology begin to impinge as we look at the constraints within which the HSPM operates; these are not linguistic constraints, but are cognitive constraints on how we decode publicly determined objects. Language, that is, exists in an intersubjective space, and in this sense we literally do not 'stop at our skins': it is precisely language, subsisting intersubjectively, which allows us to reach beyond our private existence.

Exactly how interaction between autonomous linguistic objects and speaker-internal phenomena takes place is something that needs to be investigated in an interactionist programme, but that, of course, is what the research programme is set up to establish. Much research into natural language within artificial intelligence is therefore concerned with the interface between the public and the cognitive. A further example of how we can go about establishing the nature of such interactions is the study of the relationship between numeral systems and number in Hurford (1988); it seems to me that this sort of work allows us progress in research and discovery because it is based on the idea that both numeral systems and numbers are emergent rather than Platonic or straightforwardly physical. And, with this sort of approach, we have a richer basis for proceeding with such research than we do with Botha's (1979) idea (see 4.1) that somehow we can find specific neurons that will correspond directly with postulated linguistic objects. Popper's framework suggests that the picture is ontologically much more complex than this, and that such a reductionism would fail adequately to reflect the richly articulated nature of the relationship between physical systems, cognitive systems, and products of cognitive systems.

By adopting an ontology along the lines of Popper's proposals, we avoid the pitfalls of reductionism (oversimplification, impoverished conception of ontological diversity) and the excesses of Platonism (excessive ontological diversity, absence of a conception of emergent realities: see 6.1). This provides us with a potentially fruitful way of interpreting, and building, our theories. In the following sections, I try to show it can be sustained, and, in part II, I examine this position in the light of existing responses to the ontological question.

2.4   Generalisations: the link between autonomism and realism

In discussing realism, we saw that any scientific discipline is concerned with theory construction and that its results are heavily theory-dependent. If we adopt the Popperian view of science as being characterised by falsification and deductive method, it is clear that the generalisations formulated by the theorist are of central importance. More strongly, the generalisations expressed in a theory *constitute* the theory; a scientific theory is a set of generalisations and the consequences which follow from them. Generalisations, then, are central to science. Furthermore, distinctions between classes of generalisation also enable us to distinguish one discipline from another: biochemistry is distinct from physics inasmuch as biochemical generalisations are not strictly the generalisations of physics, and cognitive psychology is distinct from either inasmuch as its generalisations are not those of biochemistry or physics. We can also note that generalisations in theoretical linguistics do not concern events, and are thus distinct from the law-like generalisations of physics.

This point is made rather well by Fodor (1982),[1] concerning the status of what he refers to as 'the special sciences'. Fodor's point concerns psychological theory, considered as a 'special science' (a specialised discipline which has emerged with the development of science), in relation to physical theory. Fodor argues convincingly (see 4.3 for details) that, even if the specific events subsumable under a generalisation in one of the special sciences are all statable in a purely physical vocabulary, this would be uninteresting. What is interesting is whether the generalisation itself is thus statable. He suggests that it is highly unlikely that the generalisations of, for instance, cognitive psychology are statable in a purely physical vocabulary, since the psychological kinds referred to in a theory of psychology are highly unlikely to correspond to physical kinds (this is his objection to type physicalism: 4.3 again for details).

Special sciences, argues Fodor, are characterised by their possession of generalisations peculiar to their domains. Thus, even if we *could* describe each instantiation of an economic generalisation in purely physical terms, the combined set of descriptions arrived at would not express the generalisation; it is the special science generalisation which allows us to specify the respects in which two physical descriptions *count* as instantiations of a generalisation:

It seems to me (to put the point quite generally) that the classical construal of the unity of science has really badly misconstrued the goal of scientific reduction. The point of reduction is not primarily to find some natural kind predicate of physics coextensive with each kind predicate of a special science. It is, rather, to explicate the physical mechanisms whereby events conform to the laws of the special sciences. I have been arguing that there is no logical or epistemological reason why success in the second of these projects should require success in the first, and that the two are likely to come apart in fact wherever the physical mechanisms whereby events conform to a law are heterogeneous. (Fodor 1981:138)

This line of argument carries over into AL: just as there are cognitive psychological generalisations which are not physical generalisations, so there are linguistic generalisations which are not cognitive psychological. Generalisations about preferred readings of ambiguous strings are cognitive psychological; generalisations about the strings and the ambiguities in themselves are linguistic. Generalisations about rules and sentences are linguistic; generalisations about utterances in context fall outside of the domain of the purely linguistic. There are also phonological generalisations which are not phonetic, and this fact alone guarantees that phonology is a discipline distinct from phonetics; it is a strictly linguistic discipline, whereas phonetics is not. More generally, we can establish the autonomy of a discipline by asking whether it deals in generalisations particular to it, and this is the case for AL.

Thus, generalisations provide us with an important link between the methodological concerns of the realist and the autonomist response to the ontological question: if they are our means of picking out properties of a theory-external reality, then we are justified in postulating a linguistic reality which our linguistic generalisations describe. Note that, allowing for a substitution of 'generalisation' for Fodor's 'law', on the assumption that linguistic phenomena are not events, the objects of theoretical linguistic activity can indeed be said to have 'come apart from' the physical and cognitive processes that gave rise to them. It is this state of affairs that an objectivist ontology recognises.

2.5   Chomsky on realism and the object of inquiry

If a realist philosophy of linguistics is combined with this objectivist ontology, it is interesting to ask in what respects it is distinct from Chomsky's version of realism, with its psychologistic ontology. That Chomsky would describe himself as a realist is self-evident, but what is interesting is the question of what this amounts to for Chomsky. He frequently cites theory construction in physics as the model upon which theories in linguistics are tested and developed, and assumes that realism is the norm in the philosophy of physics. Thus, arguing against the adoption of an instrumentalist philosophy of linguistics, he says:

to say that linguistics is the study of introspective judgements would be like saying that physics is the study of meter readings, photographs and so on, but nobody says that. Actually people did say that during the heyday of operationalism, but that did not have a pernicious effect on physics, because even the people who said it did not really believe it at any relevant level, and they did their work anyhow. At any rate, it did not make any sense, and was rapidly discarded. (Chomsky 1982:33)

As the discussions of the instrumentalist tradition in the philosophy of science in 1.2 shows, this misrepresents both the content and the history of instrumentalism. Not only was such a philosophy of science not 'rapidly discarded', it is still alive and well (see van Fraassen 1980 for a recent formulation of the principal instrumentalist arguments). Thus, Chomsky's idea that physics enjoys a universally accepted realist interpretation is quite mistaken. So too is his claim that instrumentalism 'does not make any sense': as we saw in 2.1, instrumentalist arguments against realism are rather powerful and must be met by realists.

Non-realist philosophies of sciences are only crudely summed up in the way that Chomsky describes them, but so too are their realist counterparts. Chomsky assumes, for example, that the restriction of the data of theoretical linguistics to intuitive (in his terminology, 'introspective')[2] grammaticality judgements is a consequence of the adoption of a non-realist philosophy of linguistics:

> It seems absurd to restrict linguistics to the study of introspective judgements, as is very commonly done ... many textbooks that concentrate on linguistic argumentation for example are more or less guided by that view. They offer special sets of techniques for dealing with particular data and thus reduce the field to problem solving, defining the field in these terms. That is perhaps the natural definition if you abandon any realist conception of the field. (Chomsky 1982:33–4)

In adopting the version of autonomism given in 2.3, we see that Chomsky is conflating several different issues here. When one speaks of 'the study of intuitive judgements', one must distinguish between three distinct approaches. In the first, one would allow that our object of inquiry is something over and above any set of grammaticality judgements, but, in this approach, we accept that such judgements are the principal data on which we test our theories. Under this approach, we claim, not that theoretical linguistics has grammaticality judgements as its *object* of study, but that these are its *data*, its evidential basis. This is completely in accordance with what realism is all about, and is indeed the approach adopted here.

In the second approach, in contradistinction to the first, we deny that there is some object of study over and above the data, and then restrict the data to grammaticality judgements: this *is* a non-realist position, but is quite distinct from the first approach. Both of these are distinct from the third position which Chomsky says he wants to allow for (although there is little evidence that in practice he actually follows it) where we allow that evidence other than intuitive grammaticality judgements is directly available for the testing of hypotheses in theoretical linguistics. I return to this in 2.6.

Chomsky is therefore mistaken in assuming that there are only two methodological options to choose from here, an instrumentalist 'purely problem-solving' approach, and a version of realism which admits of more than grammaticality judgements as evidence. And the option which Chomsky fails to admit of (the first of the three I describe) is fully consistent with the most central realist claims.

Consider now the bearing this has on the 'E-language/I-language' distinction, and on the issue of what it is to grasp and follow a rule. Chomsky (1986:19–46) distinguishes between externalised ('E-') language, where this is a collection of 'actions or behaviours of some sort' (p. 20), and internalised ('I-') language, where this is the native speaker–hearer's internalised grammar, which for Chomsky is a system of rules. Given the sort of objectivist realism described in 2.3, there is a clear sense of linguistic object which is neither of this 'E-' sort nor of the 'I-' sort: such subjects are external, but are not events. Thus sentences and rules are external realities which give rise to utterance phenomena, rather than being *constituted* by them. Such external objects do not constitute what Chomsky refers to as 'P-languages' (p. 33) of the Platonic sort Katz (1981) discusses, as I show in 6.1.

What emerges from this Popperian kind of externalism is a picture of the nature of languages which retains the notion of rule-governedness which Chomsky has so persuasively argued for, as well as the principle of the primacy of sentences with respect to utterances, which we simply must retain in order to make sense of the object of inquiry. However, the ontological ingredient in this picture of languages allows for the public nature of linguistic objects without undermining autonomous linguistics by collapsing it into the study of 'E-languages', and without positing Platonic entities with which we cannot interact. Rather, it claims that it is the fact of interaction which warrants us in postulating such entities.

If this picture is to be sustained, it must meet the objections made to it by, on the one hand, the anti-Chomskyan case against rule-governedness and the primacy of sentences over utterances, and, on the other, Chomsky's claim that rules, and thus knowledge of language, are speaker-internal states of affairs. The former sorts of objection need not detain us here, since the denial of the primacy of sentences over utterances commits us to being unable to talk coherently about language (see 6.3 for details), and the evidence for rule-governedness is overwhelming. The latter category of objection is much more serious, and, if it cannot be met, autonomism collapses into standard Chomskyan psychologism. To tackle the objections brought by Chomsky (notably, 1986) against Kripke's (1982) case for the public nature of rules (much of which holds for Itkonen's mutual-knowledge ontology, based as it is on an adoption of the case against private languages), let us consider a particular real-life case where rules appear to have been grasped and followed.

In a questionnaire sent out annually to university applicants, a set of expressions from a language unknown to the applicants (Tagalog) requires to be analysed. Applicants are required to formulate the rules for formation of different tenses, on the basis of the data presented. Thus, given the forms *sumulat* ('wrote'), *susulat* ('will write'), *sinulat*, ('was written') and *humanap* ('looked for'), *hahanap* ('will look for'), *hinanap* ('was looked for'), the applicant is required to analyse these complex forms as consisting of the stems *sulat* and *hanap*, with infixation of *-um-* and *-in-* after the first consonant for the simple past and past passive forms respectively, and reduplication of the first syllable to form the future tense form. A somewhat distinct sort of task is required of the applicants when they are given a single form of another verb, for instance *tinawag* ('was called'), and asked what they think the Tagalog for 'called' and 'will call' would be.

The interest of the responses lies in the fact that the applicants' ability to answer questions about the morphological analysis of the complex word forms is variable, depending on their ability consciously to compare and contrast the forms presented, but ability to guess the Tagalog translations of given English expressions is much less variable: in a great many cases, the conscious analysis yields the wrong results (*-mu-* as infix in *sumulat*, for instance, or *sum-ulat* with *sum-* as prefix) but nevertheless the guess at the Tagalog translation is correct, and at variance with the consciously formulated rule for past tense formation: these applicants give *tumawag* for 'called' but at the same time fail to analyse *sumulat* as *s-um-ulat* and *humanap* as *h-um-anap*.

These applicants have, on exposure to the data, 'grasped' the rule for the past tense formation, and thus intuitively know that, given the form *tinawag*, the past tense form is *tumawag*. But this appears to happen without conscious knowledge of the sense in which the sets of forms are parallel. We can claim that the applicant in these cases has grasped the rule, and is following it in citing *tumawag* as the simple past form. The question arises whether the rule is a private state of affairs, and whether, in following it, the applicant is engaged in a private act.

Let us begin by observing the uncontroversial fact that the applicant acquires the rule without conscious knowledge of what he is doing; this creates the possibility of rule-following in the absence of the ability consciously to say what the rule is, and this is characteristic of the way in which native speakers know their languages. The applicant brings some cognitive capacity to bear in grasping the rule, and this too can be asserted uncontroversially, without asking whether this capacity is of a specifically linguistic sort. Let us then observe that the acquisition of this rule in this case appears to have happened privately, as a result of an interaction between applicant and data. It would appear that the grasping and following of the rule takes place in this case solely as a consequence of the applicant beginning in an initial state and then, on exposure to the data, entering a final state of knowing the rule.

Now, Kripke's (1982) exposition of the Wittgensteinian sceptical problem concerning rules can be expressed thus: although we feel that it is perfectly reasonable to speak of someone's having grasped a rule and thereafter following it, there appear to be no facts about an individual that constitute being in a state of having and following a rule. There seems no way of responding to the sceptic's objection that an individual, whom we take to be following a given rule, might not be following the rule in question, that what we take that individual to mean by 'plus' might not be subdivisible into past uses of 'plus' and future uses which accord with a different rule (by which additions of numbers greater than 57 will result in 5, for instance). The sceptic's point is that we give our responses to addition exercises 'without justification'; as Kripke puts it, 'there appear to be no facts about an individual in virtue of which he accords with his past intentions' (1982:89).

Kripke's exposition of the Wittgensteinian 'sceptical solution' to this problem is intended to show that we can make sense of the notion 'following a rule' only if we cease to consider the individual in isolation. We may judge an individual to be correctly following a rule if he behaves as we would, if he gives the responses which we would. That is, rule-following can be said to exist only where there is intersubjective agreement in a community as to what would constitute a correct response. It is this observation that constitutes an argument against private rule-following and incorporates the Wittgensteinian notion of an 'independent check' on our responses, such that it is the independent check, rather than our memory of how we behaved on past occasions, which is crucial to the following of a rule. This claim is not undermined by the Robinson Crusoe case, Kripke points out, since Crusoe just happens to be physically isolated, and it is not *the fact of isolation* which prevents us from talking of rule-following, but the individual *considered in isolation*.

Chomsky's (1986:221–43) response to this is to claim that the sceptic's objection amounts to a version of general Humean scepticism concerning the underdetermination of theories by data: that we cannot cite facts about individuals which justify our attributing rule-following behaviour to them need not prevent us from making the theoretical move, as realist linguists, of thus postulating possession by the individual of rules, and postulating rule-following. And this theoretical move has its atheoretical counterpart: the attribution of rule-following behaviour to other speakers, and the abducing of the rules in question, despite their underdetermination by the utterances to which the speaker is exposed. Chomsky further claims that the Wittgensteinian is forced to attribute rule-following in just the same unjustified manner: where Crusoe gives responses we would not ourselves give, and is not interacting with a wider community, we still attribute rule-following to him, in the absence of responses which we ourselves would give. This situation in which the responses of others are not those that we ourselves would give is the norm, Chomsky claims: thus the Crusoe case is simply an exotic instance of what is the normal case.

The only sense in which a 'wider community' must be referred to, Chomsky (1986:234–5) says, is the sense in which each member of the community possesses an in-built ability to abduce rules. This sense, whereby principles of universal grammar are 'programmed in', corresponds to Pateman's (1987) 'distributed' (vs. 'collective') agreement: the property in question happens to be distributed across the members of the community simply because it is part of what constitutes our nature.

Where does this leave our example concerning the applicant? The response the applicant gives takes place, let us say, in the privacy of the applicant's isolated response to the question, and he does, as Chomsky suggests, simply follow the rule blindly, without any need for independent intersubjective checks.

The case for grasping a rule, for abducing a rule, privately is thus rather strong. But allowing that these are private states of affairs does not commit us to allowing that the rules themselves are not intersubjective, and I want to suggest that they are, and must be by definition. We are able to make sense of the notion of private rule abduction, but it is rather peculiar to say of a given algorithm that it is a rule if it is followed by only one individual.

Let us imagine that, in the entire Tagalog-speaking community, one individual alone has an algorithm for forming past tenses by infixing -*mu*- after the first syllable of the stem, rather than infixing -*um*- after first consonant, thus yielding *sumulat* and *hamunap*. This individual's behaviour can be taken to be rule-governed in that it is regular: in each case where we would expect the infix -*um*- in one postion, we notice he infixes -*mu*- in another. Now, this sense we gain of the 'rule' which the speaker is following stems from our in-built ability to attribute rule-following to others, and to abduce the rules in question. It is because of these abilities, we may speculate, that new rules can emerge. But we cannot say of such cases that a new rule *has* emerged until it holds for more than one member of a community. Once this happens, and a novel algorithm, say for past tense formation, is abduced and then followed, we may say that a new rule exists: it is that which is shared intersubjectively by this plurality of individuals.

Thus, a given form of behaviour can be taken atheoretically to constitute rule-following even where it is unique to an individual, but, unless that which is followed is shared, it is not a linguistic rule: the algorithm in question could not be said to be a rule of a language, but could only be said to describe what it is about this individual which constitutes the extent of his not knowing the language. The speaker in this case must still have the same root morphemes as his fellow speakers, and must still have an internalisation of the public rule for past tense formation (since he would no doubt be able to decode standard past tense forms). His behaviour, however, may be said to be aberrant to the extent that he fails to utilise the public rule in encoding past tense forms. In order to express what is going on here, we must state that the algorithm he follows is not a rule of a language.

This separation of public rules from the private fact of rule abduction, and from the attribution of rule-following to others, allows us to see that rule-following is a product of the interaction of the public and the private: in following a rule, we are engaged in an act which has both a private and a public aspect. It is public in that rules are necessarily intersubjective: they are what constitute our being able to communicate, where communication presupposes intersubjectivity. However, it is private in that our ability to abduce a public rule and then to follow what we abduce can come into play without any need for independent checks. We may also, apparently, simply invent new algorithms privately, and this is no doubt what is happening in the case cited by Pateman (1987:68–9) of the 'home signing' systems adopted by the deaf children of hearing, non-signing parents.

Thus we may say that the Tagalog-acquiring child, on exposure to the sorts of partial data given in the questionnaire, abduces the rule, but that the rule *per se* is not constituted as the speaker-internal state of affairs which results from this abduction. Rather, the rule exists as a state of affairs for a community, and not for an individual. Thus, what the speaker possesses is either (i) an abduced *internalisation*, or representation, of an existing rule, and not a rule *per se*, or (ii) an abduced or invented algorithm which does not correspond to a public rule, and thus cannot properly be called a linguistic rule until such time as it functions intersubjectively within a community.

This conception of the ontological diversity of rules and our abduction and internalisation of them also has consequences for the way we interpret the notion idiolect: idiolects, far from being sets of individual rules, are composite sets of internalisations of public rules within an individual: each rule, we may say, will be shared with *some* community, even though not every rule will be shared by the *same* community.

One of the benefits of this application of Popperian ontological pluralism to the nature of linguistic objects is that it allows us to begin to spell out the complex nature of the interaction between speaker-internal and speaker-external states of affairs such that we can maintain the insights of the Chomskyan conception of what it is to know a language while accommodating the Wittgensteinian insight into the public nature of rules. In doing so, we avoid a dispositionalist account of what it is to know a language, as well as the use-based conception of languages to which Itkonen (1978) is committed. We can then see why the generative enterprise, founded on the sentence/utterance distinction, can function to allow us new insights into the nature of human language without recourse to cognitive psychological evidence or to a conception of languages as collections of utterances.

2.6   The evidential basis: some objections to autonomism

The version of autonomism proposed here assumes that grammaticality judgements supply the appropriate evidence for the testing of linguistic hypotheses. Stronger still, I suggest that this is evidentially both necessary and sufficient for such testing. Against this, one could object in principle to the idea of accepting intuitive grammaticality judgements as evidence, as Botha (1979) and Sampson (1976) do (see 4.1 for discussion of Botha's position). Another position in opposition to autonomism is that of Chomsky (apparently) and Bresnan, who object to allowing *only* these as the means of directly testing linguistic hypotheses. Let us consider both of these sorts of objection.

In Chomsky's case, we find the rather odd situation in which he allows that other sorts of evidence are relevant to testing but never in practice uses, or recognises, such evidence. The state of affairs supports autonomism, however: Chomsky may deny that AL is worth pursuing but the facts of his practice show that this is precisely what he is pursuing. In contrast with Chomsky, Bresnan's (1978 and elsewhere) position has the merit of allowing that evidence from neighbouring disciplines (principally, psychology) should enter the testing of hypotheses in theoretical linguistics, and then in practice trying to develop linguistic theories which, in her view, fit the psychological evidence.

However, it is interesting to observe that in attempting to develop such a 'realistic' linguistic theory, Bresnan does pretty well what one would predict she would do if the methodological basis of our Popperian version of autonomism (not to mention Itkonen's) were right. Consider the basic contention of her lexical functional grammar (LFG) and its relation to the form and testing of the grammar. She says that psychological evidence points to a (mental) lexicon which is much more than a repository of linguistically arbitrary information, and therefore constructs a grammar in which a highly structured lexicon plays a major part. But the motivation for a grammar with a more highly structured lexicon need not be psychologically orientated, as is shown by the existence of such work as Mohanan (1986). Furthermore, it is not clear that Bresnan uses psychological evidence *directly* to test her linguistic hypotheses; in Bresnan *et al* (1982), the purely linguistic argumentation takes place separately from its supporting psychological evidence. Nor is it clear that the evidence does not equally support competing linguistic theories which do not claim to be essentially psychologically orientated. And, given the vast armament of theoretical devices being used in LFG, it would be surprising if the psychological evidence did not support *some* proportion of the framework.

The point that should be stressed about Bresnan's 'psychologically real' grammar concerns the relationship between one's metatheoretical orientation and the form of one's theory. There is no doubt that the form of one's theory is informed by one's metatheoretical assumptions (thus the importance of the issues discussed here), and this is as true for Bresnan's grammatical theory as it is of any other. What needs to be demonstrated by Bresnan is that *only* her metatheoretical position, to the exclusion of other competing positions (such as Itkonen's, or Katz's, or the one proposed here), gives rise to the sort of grammatical theory she proposes. If this is not the case, and one suspects that it is not, then there is no reason to take linguistic evidence in support of her theory to count as a vindication of her particular metatheoretical approach.

All of this suggests that, if one considers LFG (as a grammatical framework) and its motivation independently, Bresnan can be seen to be carrying out two distinct activities. The first of these is standard autonomous linguistic hypothesising and testing, carried out independently of psychological evidence, and the second is psycholinguistic investigation which, far from directly testing these hypotheses, is meant to suggest that they *fit* with the available psycholinguistic evidence. The non-psychological realism adopted here would lead us to expect precisely this sort of relationship between autonomous linguistics and psycholinguistics. In short, Bresnan is practising AL and the adducing psychological evidence which has some degree of fit with the grammatical framework she has elaborated. But this does not amount to testing the grammar directly with psycholinguistic evidence. It would appear that the Popperian objectivist framework I adopt characterises rather accurately the actual practice of both Chomsky and Bresnan.

Sampson's (1976) objection to autonomism is that grammaticality judgements do not constitute an evidential basis which is something other than a set of events. Well-formed expressions, he claims, are interpretable as that which we would normally utter in context, all things being equal, and those acts of uttering are events. We are concerned, therefore, with that which can be characterised as a normal event, and thus with laws governing those events. This, he claims, is paralleled in natural science, where we consider events that normally happen, all things being equal, and the laws that govern them. Were things not equal, Sampson says, we could be made to utter anything (if a loaded revolver were held to our temple, for instance).

This does not undermine our case for the evidential basis as something over and above events, however. Consider the situation in which a revolver is indeed held to one's temple in order to extract an anomalous utterance from the speaker. Here, Sampson claims that our *ceteris paribus* clause must be appealed to to rule out the anomalous event as not being covered by the laws we have adduced. But we require to know what it is that the person with the revolver knows which allows him to know what to demand of the speaker. Clearly, the person with the revolver must know what counts as well-formed and ill-formed before any demand for an utterance of an ill-formed expression can be made.

Now *this* forces us to concede the point which Sampson denies. The revolver, and thus the idea of a *ceteris paribus* clause concerning events, is neither here nor there: what counts is simply the knowledge of ill-formedness and well-formedness, and of course our person with the revolver accesses this intuitively. The ill-formed expression which the person with the revolver demands to be uttered is not an event, even if any instance of its being uttered is. Rather than being events, well-formed expressions, and the rules which define them, are those things which allow us to characterise utterance events. In postulating the existence of these rules and expressions, we are able to express the properties of the expression (a sentence or some subpart of a sentence) of which an utterance is an instantiation.

The arguments that intuitively accessed grammaticality judgements either are not sufficient or are not necessary as the evidential basis for linguistic theory cannot proceed, and the fact of theoretical linguistic practice shows that autonomous linguistics proceeds with such evidence being not only necessary but also sufficient for the testing of hypotheses.

Before we leave this question of the evidential basis of AL and proceed to consider objections to realism in the philosophy of linguistics, it is as well to respond briefly to a frequently voiced but unworrying objection concerning grammaticality judgements as evidence. It is at times pointed out that there are cases of 'asterisk fade', where intuitive responses supply us with a gradient scale of well-formed to ill-formed expressions. The objection is that the evidence here contains grey areas and that the ill-formed vs. well-formed distinction upon which AL rests is thus undermined.

A moment's reflection shows that, far from undermining the distinction, asterisk fade *presupposes* it: one cannot coherently speak of a cline from well-formed to ill-formed without a clear conception of what these are. Furthermore, once we have erected a set of theoretical proposals to deal with the ill-formed and well-formed cases, the theory itself will allow us to decide on the status of asterisk-faded expressions, as Chomsky has long since observed.

It appears that arguments against autonomism from the nature of the evidential basis are not well-founded. What we must proceed to consider now is whether the realist element of this philosophy of linguistics is tenable, that is, whether an instrumentalist philosophy of linguistics serves equally well as a metatheory for linguistic inquiry.

3 *Instrumentalism in linguistics*

3.1 Introduction

Having examined (in 1.2) some of the main instrumentalist arguments against realism, I now want to look at some of the interpretations of an instrumentalist sort which have been made of constructs in linguistic theory, at aspects of what might be called 'the instrumentalist tradition' in theoretical linguistics. The first of these is in pre-generative structuralist linguistics of the sort carried out in the United States in the 1930s and 1940s (another term might be Bloomfieldian and post-Bloomfieldian linguistics). Here the influence of logical positivism is apparent; I examine some of its most central claims and try to assess the extent of its influence on the methodology of linguists working within this period. The second is a more recent, and generally more sophisticated, set of assertions about the way in which we should interpret our theoretical constructs: those made by Lass (1976, 1980 and elsewhere), as reflected in his view of our constructs as 'uninterpreted calculus'. Finally, I examine interesting instrumentalist elements in the work of Itkonen, which I return to in my discussion of his views in 5.1.

3.2 Structuralism and logical positivism

The importance attached to observability which figures so prominently in the instrumentalist challenge to realism is very much apparent in, and in fact constitutes much of the basis of, the logical positivist philosophy of science. A central component of their set of proposals was an attempt to demonstrate that metaphysical propositions are not meaningful, that the only meaningful propositions are those that are elementary and correspond to simple facts of observation, or those that are more complex than this, but which are constructed out of a series of elementary propositions via the logical operations, such that their truth or falsehood is entirely dependent on the truth or falsehood of the elementary statements in question, the elementary statements being expressed wholly in observation language. They also held that such elementary propositions are empirically verifiable, and that we gain knowledge via this process of building up meaningful propositions out of elementary empirically verifiable statements. It follows from this that when we attempt to communicate via metaphysical statements, which are not so constructed, we literally fail to communicate at all: we have not said anything meaningful (i.e. we have said nothing; note the similarity between this and the Wittgensteinian private language argument: whereas metaphysical assertions might reflect some sort of inner state of the speaker, they cannot be said to be meaningful, where meaning is intersubjective).

These fundamental doctrines of logical positivism, as expressed by the members of the Vienna Circle (such as Schlick, Carnap, and Neurath), can be seen as constituting an alternative to realism when one considers the proposition 'there is a transcendent external world'. Since this is not reducible to a set of elementary observational statements, it must be taken to be a metaphysical assertion. As such, it is taken to be meaningless within the logical positivist approach. Schlick (1959) was at pains to point out that they were not *denying* the existence of an external world, but were saying that such assertions, and also their negations, were meaningless metaphysics, that in asserting them we assert nothing. This is, for instance, what Carnap's 'criterion of significance' states: only statements in observation language are meaningful, and that which cannot be reduced to observation language has no meaning.

This philosophy of science runs into the problems discussed in chapter 1 concerning the observation/theory distinction. Note that the distinction can lead to a version of sensationalism such as Mach's very easily, since the notion 'physical object' can be objected to by saying that the proposition 'there are external physical objects' is just as metaphysical as 'there is an external physical world'; all we have as a certain basis for our knowledge are observation experiences, which are sense experiences. Consider Mach's comment that our theoretical constructs are best interpreted as devices for stating as economically as possible sets of laws about our sense experiences: 'Properly speaking, the world is not composed of "things" as its elements, but of colours, tones ... in short, what we call individual sensations ... the whole affair [of constructing a physical theory] is a mere affair of economy' (Mach 1966:579).

An interesting consequence of taking this line is that it ends up in a philosophy which becomes increasingly solipsistic: the only foundation for our knowledge is our subjective sense experiences. There are a couple of ways of attempting to avoid this conclusion and still retaining positivism, however. One is Russell's (1908), in which a distinction is made between the content of our sense experiences as individuals (these are distinct even in those circumstances when two or more individuals might be said to be perceiving the same object) and what he calls their structure, by which he means the circumstances under which they occur; it is this which is remarkably similar from one individual to another. This is no real solution to the problem, though, since it is impossible to tell that the circumstances under which our shared sense experiences occur are similar unless one makes the metaphysical leap of simply asserting that this is so in order to make sense of our reports of sense experiences. A more workable solution is Schlick's, which is to avoid saying that physical bodies are 'complexes of sensations', and to say instead that 'propositions concerning bodies are transformable into equivalent propositions concerning the occurrence of sensations in accordance with laws' (1959:107), so that the subject-matter of a physical theory is not sensations, but laws. As a way out of Mach's solipsistic sensationalism, which is a fair way down the road to idealism, this is certainly an improvement on Russell.

Obviously, the problem will not arise if one adopts the realist position of chapter 1: we can assume, with Quine, that both the notions 'physical world' and 'physical object' are myths which allow us a great amount of progress in managing our experiences, and we can add the realist argument that, unless we assume that there really are physical objects and a physical world, there would be no account of why these notions should do so much work for us. As Popper has repeatedly pointed out, a major factor in favour of realism is that it allows us to maintain the objectivity of science, while positivism sees it diminish into, at best, laws about our sense experiences.

Regarding the claim that metaphysical propositions are literally meaningless: this has been adequately countered by Popper, whose demarcation criterion distinguishes falsifiable from non-falsifiable theories while not proposing this as a criterion of meaningfulness. What seems to have emerged as a consensus, among realists and non-realists alike, is the view that our theories do have an irreducibly metaphysical ingredient, whether one refers to this in terms of metaphysical research programmes underlying theories, or theories themselves as metaphors. The logical positivist attempt to divorce scientific theories from metaphysical assumptions can be said to have failed.

However, it is clear from the discussion in 1.2 that some of the core notions of this sort of 'consistent empiricism' (as it was also known: see Schlick 1959) can be developed into sophisticated instrumentalist arguments which do seriously oppose realism. What I intend here is not, therefore, a critique of logical positivism, but an examination of the effects of logical positivism on the methodology of linguistic analysis in the United States in the 1930s and 1940s, much of which is important because it forms the methodological background against which generative principles were formulated.

In talking about the influence of positivist thought upon linguistics, I am not concerned with establishing that, say, Bloomfield or Harris read and was consciously guided by the works of the Vienna Circle. Rather, I want to suggest that many of the central ideas of positivism came to constitute a general intellectual climate of opinion concerning the nature of science (Miller 1973 makes this point very clearly) and that this had important repercussions for the way in which linguistic analysis was carried out (and, of course, this in turn had consequences for the way in which generative work was done).

An interesting statement of an instrumentalist methodology for linguistic analysis comes from Twaddell's (1958) paper on possible interpretations of the 'phoneme' construct. Having started with an argument from idealisation (that we arrive at the phoneme via abstraction from a corpus of data), he asserts that:

The macro-phoneme is a fiction, defined for the purpose of describing conveniently the phonological relations among the elements of a language, its forms. The sum of such relations among the elements is the phonological system of the language. This phonological system is of course nothing objectively existent: it is not definable as a mental pattern in the minds of the speakers of the language; it is not even a 'Platonic idea' which the language actualises ... The phonological system is the phonetician's and phonologist's summarised formulation of the relations; it is not a phenomenon, nor an intuition. (1953:76)

This paper is interesting because of its rejection of even a physical definition of the phoneme, which represents the consensus view among structuralists of the period and is itself largely influenced by positivist physicalism. The rejection of a psychological interpretation is typical of the positivist-influenced work of the time: the idea that science is concerned with observables is here interpreted such that mental phenomena are taken to be unobservable and therefore not the proper concern of the scientist. Of course, logical positivists themselves did not assume that mental phenomena were not a proper object of scientific inquiry; rather, they assumed that notions such as 'mental' were reducible to statements concerning observable behavioural phenomena: here we see how the legacy of positivism helped mould methodological trends, rather than functioning as the explicitly adopted scientific method for linguistic inquiry.

Many of the instrumentalist arguments against realism can be seen in Twaddell's methodological position: pragmatism (stressing the purpose of the investigator), the denial that theoretical constructs have theory-external referents, the emphasis on patterns and relations among the phenomena. But note the extent to which Twaddell cannot help but incorporate a realist ingredient into this instrumentalism: he allows himself to talk of relations and (phonological) forms in a realist manner. If the phonological system is nothing which actually exists, and if it is the sum of the relations among the forms, are we to conclude that the relations and forms themselves are not objective realities? Must we assume that we can legitimately speak of the existence of forms and the relations between them, assuming that any theoretical statement is reducible to a statement about forms and their relations, and not anything over and above these?

An affirmative answer would seem to accord with Schlick's reductionist position, and is open to the usual objections to reductionism: one cannot help smuggling theoretical concepts into the picture (recall Putnam's 1962 point that, even in the most 'observational' of statements, terms like 'physical object' appear), and these themselves are used in a realist way: Twaddell speaks of relations as if they were observable, but they are in fact abstractions of the very sort that he wishes to assume no ontological commitment to. Thus he would be forced, in order to maintain a consistent instrumentalism, to allow that even his 'observables' are abstractions, and would have to retreat to some kind of solipsistic position, taking the only realities to be sense experiences.

I have concentrated here on what I think are the weakest points in Twaddell's methodological position; it should be pointed out that his arguments against physicalism and psychologism are impressive (it is interesting, given subsequent historical developments in the philosophy of linguistics, that he considers a Platonistic interpretation of the phoneme construct). My main point is that, in abandoning these, and in appreciating the fact that our constructs do not correspond in any simple way to extra-theoretical entities, one need not embrace instrumentalism as the only remaining alternative. This is, in fact, precisely the point I want to make about the work of Lass and Itkonen on the subject.

It is this combination of a non-instrumentalist methodology coupled with an autonomy thesis of the sort proposed by Lass (1980) that constitutes the main thrust of my proposals; it is a combination which has been overlooked. As evidence that it has indeed been overlooked, consider Twaddell's conclusion that the construct 'phoneme' cannot be said to correspond to a physical, to a psychological, or to a Platonic reality, and his assumption that we must therefore adopt an instrumentalist position. My proposals show that these do not exhaust the available options. The same can be said about Katz's (1981) proposals (6.1): he assumes that, if we abandon instrumentalism and psychologism, Platonism is the only option left open.

To return to structuralist linguistics: it may be argued that Twaddell is not wholly representative of the instrumentalist position in structuralist methodology; since, as Joos (1958:80) points out, his position on the interpretation of the phoneme was not widely adopted, it is perhaps best to examine the views of Bloomfield, and later those of Harris, as being more representative of the period.

Bloomfield's methodological views generally represent a much more thoroughly positivist position than those of Twaddell, incorporating a version of physicalism very similiar to that of the logical positivists. However, as Itkonen (1978:70) has pointed out, Bloomfield did not subscribe to the view, held by Twaddell and Harris, that a corpus of utterances constitutes the data base for linguistic analyses, and, in this respect, his philosophy of linguistics is less positivist than it might have been.

We can see the extent of the influence positivism had on Bloomfield's methodology in this statement: 'The only useful generalisations about language are inductive generalisations ... when we have adequate data about many languages, we shall have to return to the problem of general grammar ... but this study, when it comes, will not be speculative but inductive' (Bloomfield 1935:20). This is in stark contrast to Chomsky's views on the matter, and is linked to Bloomfield's reductivist insistence that every structural unit postulated by the linguist must be reducible to some physical phenomenon; take, for example, his definition of the phoneme as 'A minimum same of vocal feature is a phoneme or distinctive sound' (Bloomfield 1926:27). Thus, inductivism and reductivist physicalism constitute the core of Bloomfield's methodology. I argue in 6.3 that this physical interpretation of phonological objects has survived and is as difficult to sustain now as it was in Bloomfield's time.

I will not concentrate on Bloomfield's statements as to linguistic meaning in relation to stimulus–response behaviourism, which has been adequately criticised elsewhere (see Itkonen 1978:68–71 for some interesting criticism). I do want to point out, in passing, that some of the early work in generative phonology assumed an interpretation of phonological objects remarkably similar to Bloomfield's. Thus, Jakobson and Halle (1968) demand that 'any distinctive feature and, consequently, any phoneme treated by the linguist, have its constant correlate at each stage of the speech event and thus be identifiable at any level accessible to observation'.

If Bloomfield's views are unnecessarily burdened with positivist assumptions, it is interesting to consider the views of Harris, whose work is commonly taken to constitute the historical link between stucturalist and generative linguistics. Unlike Bloomfield, and like Twaddell, Harris takes the data of linguistic theory to be observable events, or regularities among those events, selected from a corpus. The data, for him, are behavioural:

Investigation in descriptive linguistics consists of recording utterances in a single dialect and analysing the recorded material. The stock of recorded utterances constitutes the corpus of data, and the analysis which is made of it is a compact description of the distribution of elements within it. (Harris 1963:12)

In investigations in descriptive linguistics, linguistic elements are associated with particular features of the speech behaviour in question, and the relations among these elements are studied. (p. 17)

As we have seen from the discussion of Sampson's interpretation of linguistic evidence as observable events, the proposals as to the corpus-based nature of theoretical linguistic inquiry are viable as a description neither of how work ought to proceed in theoretical linguistics, nor of how it actually does proceed. But consider also the relationship which Harris takes to hold between what he takes to be the 'observable data' and the theoretical constructs we devise to account for them. For Harris, these are merely 'symbols' upon which operations can be performed:

However, in the course of reducing our elements to simpler combinations of more fundamental elements, we set up entities such as junctures and long components which can only with difficulty be considered as variables directly representing any member of a class of portions of the flow of speech. It is therefore more convenient to consider the elements as purely logical symbols, upon which various operations of mathematical logic can be performed. (Harris 1963:18)

This reflects most of the instrumentalist preoccupations of the logical positivists, and all of their shortcomings. It is an attempt to separate theoretical from observational terms and to avoid ontological commitment to the former. Against it, we may argue that this separation is impossible, and that, if constructs like 'long' and 'juncture' are heuristically fertile, this is sufficient warrant for granting them 'real' status. We can claim that languages do actually have length as a functioning property of their rules, and that the temporal length we perceive is a manifestation of this (Árnason 1980 uses the terms 'quantity' and 'length', respectively, to distinguish these). If we find that constructs such as 'juncture phoneme' do not have the heuristic fertility of their constructs, then we are justified in abandoning them in favour of others, which in turn we are warranted in claiming 'real' status for.

It is fairly widely accepted now, of course, that American structuralist linguistics was limited in its ability to express linguistically significant generalisations; what is of interest to us is that these limitations followed from the non-realist metatheory upon which it was built. The generative enterprise, with its realist metatheory, created new avenues of theoretical research largely because of its distinct methodological starting-point.

However, with the introduction of a specifically psychological realism, the question of how the expression 'psychologically real' might be interpreted arose. Objections to the purported psychological reality of linguistic constructs were thus potentially interpretable as objections to realism *per se*, even though we are not committed, in rejecting the former, to rejecting the latter. I suggest that realism also became less attractive to some because naive realist claims about, for instance, the reality of particular constructs (such as specific transformational rules) came to be made. 'When did transformations appear in the emergence of language?', 'What are the transformations of German?', and 'Does the passive transformation exist?' became questions that seemed reasonable to some. We saw in 2.1 that we need only insist on a realist interpretation of the falsifiable claims expressed by entire analyses (the rules and the representations taken together), rather than of specific rules. Particular phrase structure or transformational rules do not, in and of themselves, express falsifiable claims for which realist interpretations may be given.

But this point was not, I suggest, always appreciated, and one suspects that it was in reaction to the sort of naive realism implicit in such questions that Lass (1976, 1980) began to elaborate a metatheoretical position which contained elements of instrumentalism and stressed the power of our constructs to shape our perception of the object of inquiry. I look now at his proposals.

3.3   Uninterpreted calculus

The instrumentalism in Lass's work can be traced from as far back as Lass and Anderson (1975) and then down through Lass (1976) to Lass (1980), where it finds its fullest expression; traces of it are even apparent in his 1984 textbook on phonology, which does not dwell unduly on matters methodological. Lass's metatheoretical position has evolved somewhat since the publication of his 1980 work; I will attempt to show to what extent this development is explicable in terms of the realist/instrumentalist distinction.

In the epilogue to his 1976 work, Lass adopts Popper's demarcation criterion and argues that linguistics lies on the metaphysical rather than the scientific side of the demarcation (but is none the less a rational activity); that is, he takes linguistic theories not to be falsifiable. For him this means that they are not susceptible to disconfirmation in the face of 'experience', thus: 'I think that most theories in linguistics are not in fact scientific in the strict sense, but belong to category (c) [theories which are not refutable]: linguistics is at this point largely – if not nearly exclusively – a form of philosophy or metaphysics' (Lass 1976:216). He proceeds to argue for the validity of non-refutable theories (which for him means 'non-empirical') as a valuable kind of rational activity. He suggests that we recognise them as such, and carry on with theoretical linguistics without pretending that it is an empirical science, or genuinely attempt to convert it into such a science by turning it into a properly experimental discipline, along the lines suggested by Derwing (1973) and Ohala, a move which Lass thinks would be counter-productive.[1] This statement of Lass's position in the late 1970s is, I believe, important for an understanding of the basic intent of his 1980 work, which has attracted a fairly wide range of criticisms, some of which have, I believe, misconstrued the intent of the work.

What Lass (1976) overlooks, I suggest, is that we have a third choice intermediate between empirically (based on spatiotemporal observation) testable theories and non-empirical, non-testable theories: theories which are testable, but not empirically; one can test linguistic hypotheses, but this need not be via 'experience' or the observation of spatiotemporal events.[2] It is this position, argued for in Itkonen (1978) which constitutes a fundamental part of the realist philosophy of AL given in 2.1. We have also seen (2.2) that testing of hypotheses in AL is readily interpretable as an application of deductive method, but in a non-nomic domain. I agreed there with Lass that D–N explanation was not available in AL, but I noted that it is the nomic, rather than the deductive, aspect of such explanations that is not available to us. Thus, I concluded that AL is a scientific enterprise, since its hypotheses may be falsifiable.

On the interconnection between the methodological and ontological questions, consider Lass's comments in his 1980 work, the general aim of which is to show that, if genuine scientific explanation is deductive–nomological, then historical linguistics does not have any such mode of explanation available to it.[3] He proposes, in relation to the ontological question, that it is useful to talk of 'a linguistic world three' (1980:122), by means of which we can recognise the possibility of 'language without a knowing/using speaker', parallel to Popper's epistemology without a knowing agent. This suggestion is precisely the one I have adopted and elaborated on in 2.3.

I should note at this point that, if one broadens the notion of causality to allow reasons as causes (Itkonen 1983; Adamska-Sałaciak 1986) or to allow that causal mechanisms may be said to be transfactually active, i.e. even when they are cancelled out by other mechanisms and thus do not create effects (Pateman 1987, following Bhaskar 1979), then Lass's claim that causal explanations are not available in historical linguistics can be retracted. Pateman (1987:25) correctly points out that Lass (1980) is mistaken in identifying probability statements and tendency statements; he says that, if tendencies can be identified as transfactually active causal mechanisms, then the notion 'tendency' can be allowed to count as explanatory.

But, even if Lass had not conflated tendency and probability statements, I do not see that his adopting Bhaskar's realist philosophy of science would have improved matters. I suggest below (5.2) that we should not adopt the Bhaskar/Pateman view of causal mechanisms, because it commits us to unfalsifiable hypotheses: there is simply no way of falsifying claims about transfactually active mechanisms in language. Given that this is so, it is not at all clear that the explanations they allow us are to be valued.

In tracking the development of Lass's thought on the relationship between the methodological and ontological questions, I think we find that there is a conflict between his responses to them. He allows for a Popperian 'world three' ontology of linguistic objects, but at the same time wants to deny that we should allow ourselves any commitment to their ontological status. Now, one cannot both specify their ontological status and at the same time refuse to specify it. Let us see how Lass ends up with this problem. He says that the consequences of adopting an onto-logy of knowledge without a knowing subject are something like those dis-cussed by Eddington, in which 'the study of a (putatively) "empirical" domain is not to be viewed as a "direct" study of the domain itself, but rather a study of our knowledge of it' (Eddington 1938:123). Eddington's view of physics sees it not as an investigation of an entity, the external world, which our knowledge is said to describe, but an investigation of knowledge itself. This leads to an ontology of 'pure structure', where our constructs are said by Lass to be 'uninterpreted calculus'. This seems to me an overtly instrumentalist interpretation of our constructs; it reflects the fact that Eddington was an idealist who was at pains to stress that the world consists primarily of contents of consciousness.

Consider, for instance, the passage quoted by Lass (1980:125): 'To the question: what is X when it is not a sensation in any consciousness ... the right answer is probably that the question is a meaningless one – that structure does not necessarily imply an X of which it is the structure' (Eddington 1938:151). Lass says that, with the addition of an instrumenta-list metaphysics, this reflects the metatheoretical view of Harris. But this *is* an instrumentalist metaphysics. Eddington is clearly an instrumentalist, and, in following him, Lass inherits this instrumentalism. Both believe that our theoretical frameworks cannot reasonably be taken to be about extra-theoretical entities. Lass (1980) argues that Eddington is not an idealist in the strict sense, but is simply displaying 'an acute consciousness of the power of an epistemological framework to dictate the shape of its own contents – as well as the fact that it always stands as an insuperable barrier to "direct experience" of anything (there are no theory-free obser-vation languages)' (p. 124). But Eddington's philosophy is clearly idealis-tic:

To put the conclusion crudely, the stuff of the world is mind- stuff.

The mind-stuff of the world is, of course, something more general than our indi-vidual conscious minds.

The mind-stuff is the aggregation of relations and relata which form the building material for the physical world.

It is difficult for the matter-of-fact physicist to accept the view that the substratum of everything is of *mental* character. But no-one can deny that mind is the first and most direct thing in our experience, and all else is remote inference. (Eddington 1927:281, emphasis added)

And one can stress the fact that epistemological frameworks have the power to dictate their own contents without abandoning realism. One need not see theories as barriers to the experiencing of reality, but as enabling devices which allow us to get at the structure of reality. Lass is right, of course, in stating that there can be no 'direct' experience of reality without intervening theoretical constructs, but that is partly what realism is about: the logical positivist notion of direct sensory experience and of statements reporting it was not viable as a picture of how our perceptual system works, and of how we gain knowledge of the world. By adopting the realist's argument that our theories get at reality which induces our sense experiences (see Maxwell 1962 for a statement of this sort of 'causal theory of perception'), while still allowing that the theories shape our perceptions, we avoid the subjectivist trap of saying that our theories can only be about the contents of our own consciousness (Eddington) or sense experiences (Mach, logical positivism).

It might be argued that Eddington is not committed to instrumentalism or idealism in stressing the power of our theories to shape our perceptions (I am grateful to Jim Hurford for pointing this out), and that I therefore unfairly accuse Lass of adopting an instrumentalist position. While I do not agree with Hempel (1966:77), who claims that Eddington 'denies the existence of everyday objects', I do claim that it is the notion that the theory-external world in some sense possesses a mental character that constitutes Eddington's idealism.

If one is to allow that any philosophy is idealistic (say, Berkeley's), that there are idealistic philosophies, then one must allow that certain claims about the nature of reality are idealistic. The most common one I know of (discussed in, for example, Popper 1963 and Russell 1908) is this: that the physical world is partly (even primarily) mental and that we can only speak of the existence of something if we can speak of perceiving it (*esse* = *percipere*). This is, I think, precisely what Eddington is saying. It is a position that seems to me clearly in contrast to the realist one, and has historically been taken to be so (see Popper 1963 for discussion of the historical roots of instrumentalism in idealism, particularly Berkeley's, and Putman 1975 for the view that idealism has historically been in opposition to various versions of realism).

It seems to me that Lass's (1980) avoidance of ontological commitment leaves him with a non-realist interpretation of our constructs (as uninterpreted calculus) by default. But, if 'world three' objects, as Popper (1972) describes them, are objectively existing objects, independent of our knowledge of them, then we cannot both claim that the object of inquiry exists as an autonomous reality and then *deny* that our theories about it are theories about such an objective reality. It is only by adopting a realist methodology that we can square our methodological assumptions with these ontological assumptions.

The positive contribution made by Lass (1980) is that its entire thrust is against naive realism and against the notion that linguistic theorising is describable within a D–N account of scientific explanation. But Lass, in adopting, by default, an instrumentalist interpretation of theoretical linguistic constructs, is left with the problem of squaring this with his ontological assumptions. Interestingly, with the constructivist metatheory which has evolved in his more recent work, we see what might be interpreted as concessions to realism, but with the same reluctance to allow that an ontology of linguistic objects gets us anywhere.

Lass's more recent work moves away from the non-realist 'uninterpreted calculus' view towards a version of constructivism which seeks to balance the theory-dependent nature of descriptive terms with realist assumptions. Thus, in his 1986 paper, he seeks to show how Boyd's notion of theory-constitutive metaphors may be applied to AL and historical linguistics.

We see realist assumptions appearing when he notes (1986:28) that it is important to assess the relative fruitfulness of a construct and that there is no way of understanding why one construct should be more fruitful than another except by making the realist assumption that there are properties of the object of inquiry which determine relative fruitfulness. However, Lass resists Boyd's (1973) claims about realism by stressing that there is no a priori reason why theoretical success should rest on ontological grounds. I think this leaves him with relative success as a mystery, and a conflict between his avoidance of ontological commitment and the realist element in his analysis.

Take his example of a theory-constitutive metaphor in historical linguistics: the 'Great Vowel Shift' notion and its history. Lass shows how theoretical terms such as this make the transition from 'theoretical' to 'observational' status, and allow us to say what constitutes a fact about the vowel shift. But later in the paper (1986:33) Lass states that it is 'after all beside the point to talk about the "reality" or (extratheoretical) "existence" of chain shifts as a kind, or even any particular one'. He says that

'The success of the metaphor is theory-internal (or field-internal) in that it facilitates reference to a conceptual (if not strictly "natural") kind that can be identified and even have "empirical claims" made about it.' His final remarks concerning ontological interpretation are that: (i) there is little point in trying to provide ontological specification: we should avoid basing our requirements of theories on those in sciences whose objects inhabit the spatiotemporal 'real world'; and (ii) even if a construct as theory-constitutive metaphor goes out of existence, much more is known about the object of inquiry via the process of establishing, modifying, developing hypotheses from, and arguing against such a construct.

The second of these observations is acute, and well-exemplified in his paper, but I see no reason for him to retain the non-realist position expressed in (i). While it is quite clear that linguistic realities are not of the spatiotemporal sort, as Lass observes, what we require is an extension, beyond the spatiotemporal, of what may count as a part of the real world, and vowel shifts, of either the drag-chain or push-chain sort, may reasonably be given a realist interpretation. As we have seen in 1.2, we need realist assumptions in order to make sense of why it should be that some constructs should be more fruitful than others.

Without these assumptions, we have only relativism to fall back on: theoretical constructs are merely better or worse for different purposes. It is precisely this kind of relativism which informs Itkonen's pragmatist interpretation of linguistic theories, to which I now turn.

3.4   Pragmatism

I discuss Itkonen's (1978, 1983) metatheory in detail in 5.1; here I want briefly to comment on the pragmatist interpretation of theoretical constructs which he adopts. According to Itkonen, our theoretical statements, which include our hypotheses about why the data should be as they are, are falsifiable, but are merely 'pictures' or systematisations of sets of rule-sentences, which in turn are about norms (normative rules). Furthermore, rule-sentences and hypothetical statements are about the same thing. Thus: 'non-trivial grammatical theories, whose truth or falsity is *not* known, are not empirical theories, but hypothetical conceptual descriptions, given that both (atheoretical) rule-sentences and (theoretical) grammars speak – in different ways – about the *same* normative reality' (Itkonen 1978:166, emphasis in original).

Hypotheses in AL are therefore, for Itkonen, about a reality which is normative. Itkonen accepts (1983:134–5) that we may choose, on non-arbitrary grounds, between competing linguistic theories. The choice between them, however, is, he claims, not determined by correspondence between theoretical terms and unobservable entities, as in the empirical sciences, but by whether a given theory provides us with 'a good overview of the subject'. The pragmatist element in his metatheory consists in his insisting that the criteria vary from one linguistic school to another, and this, I suggest, robs his discussion of any non-arbitrary grounds for choosing between competing theories.

He denies (1983:129) that it is even possible to talk in a non-circular way of one theory being more fertile or successful than another. This rather contradicts his comments about the growth of science in his 1978 work (p. 171), where he seems to think that believing the earth to be flat is less desirable than believing it to be round; surely this sort of comment presupposes precisely the sort of conception of success that Itkonen says we can only define circularly, i.e. in relation to arbitrarily changing purposes. From the realist point of view, the heuristic fertility of supposing the earth to be spherical is sufficient warrant for saying that it really is so, unless we come up with an even more fruitful proposal.

We saw, in discussing Quine (1.2), that the pragmatist emphasis on the purpose for which a theory is constructed becomes unhelpful if that purpose is the attempted description of reality, if it is a realist purpose. And this, Boyd (1973) claims, is usually the case in science. If we respond to this, as Duhem did, by saying that it is the scientist's activity, not his purpose, that counts, and thus diminish the role of the realist aim of science, then we must abandon pragmatism, which accepts theoretical diversity by allowing merely for differing theories for differing purposes.

But Itkonen need not be committed to conceding that purpose is irrelevant in evaluating theories. Rather, he can deny that our realist/instrumentalist distinction is relevant when it comes to assessing linguistic theories. Thus he argues that:

It is tempting to view the dichotomy of AL vs. psychologism as exemplifying the distinction between the trends in the philosophy of empirical science known as 'instrumentalism' and 'realism'. For this comparison to be valid, however, it should first be proved that AL is an empirical science. But this has not been proved. If on the contrary, AL is a nonempirical science comparable to analytical philosophy or formal logic, as I have argued all along, there is no justification for relating it to the 'intrumentalism vs. realism' issue. (1983:824–5)

In reply to this, it should be stated that we need not claim that the autonomous linguistics vs. psychologistic linguistics distinction exemplifies the instrumentalist vs. realist distinction. In fact, I want explicitly to deny that this is so. The instrumentalist vs. realist distinction is one that is applicable even if one abandons psychologism and adopts a radical autonomy thesis for theoretical linguistics; Itkonen is mistaken in assuming that an autonomy thesis is somehow intimately connected with the adoption of an instrumentalist methodology.

Further, it is clear that Itkonen supposes that one can 'prove' that AL is either an empirical or a non-empirical science. But proof is not a particularly useful notion here; on the contrary, we are dealing here with meta-scientific argumentation rather than proof. But, even if we accept Itkonen's definition of what counts as an empirical science, and agree that AL is non-empirical, and that method in theoretical linguistics proceeds the way Itkonen says it does, it does not follow that the realist/instrumentalist distinction is irrelevant to AL.

We have seen that the distinction is indeed relevant, and that the realist assumption is explanatory in an important sense: it gives us an account of the relative success of theories; it also forces us to develop our theories when they are challenged by others. If we adopt a pragmatist metatheory, we are under no such obligation; proliferation of competing theories is both expected and accepted. In theoretical linguistics, we end up, in adopting Itkonen's pragmatism, by accepting all proposed theoretical frameworks and assuming that there is nothing at issue, other than the purely pragmatic fact of one's purpose in proposing a theory, when it comes to deciding between them. This is a warrant for heuristic complacency, and is interestingly not in accord with what practitioners actually do (even if one seeks an eclectic synthesis of current theoretical proposals, one is still attempting to produce a theoretical proposal distinct from any single contributing theory, and attempting to select from the contents of individual theories what one takes to be their most fertile parts).

It seems to me that the fundamental assumptions underlying the realist position are more appropriate for theoretical linguistics than their instrumentalist rivals; in what follows, I will assume the version of realism I have described and try to tackle the ontological questions which necessarily accompany it.

II

THE ONTOLOGICAL QUESTION

4 *Linguistic objects as psychological realities*

4.1 Materialism and reductionism

Reductionism in psychology

Consider the case for materialism put by Smart (1963). He argues for a realist interpretation of (macroscopic, microscopic, and submicroscopic) terms in physics, and rejects an instrumentalist account of these in terms of sense data statements. That is, he takes it to be untenable to devise a realist interpretation of macroscopic objects and at the same time an instrumentalist or phenomenalist interpretation of submicroscopic objects (pp. 16–49). He then argues (pp. 50–63) that we must interpret terms and statements in biology and psychology (and any other 'emergent' domain of inquiry) in an entirely instrumentalist way. He therefore proposes that we reduce all statements in biology and psychology to 'genuine' law-like statements in physics. It is on these grounds that he assumes that there are no 'emergent laws and properties' (p. 52) but only 'empirical generalisations' (p. 52) in these disciplines. This follows from his physicalism: since there are only physical realities, and since physics constitutes the study of such realities, then any laws there are will be physical laws, statable solely in the terms of physics; any generalisations which can be made outside of physics are reducible to genuinely explanatory laws of physics.

It follows from this that our linguistic reality, as psychological reality, must be describable in terms of 'genuinely explanatory' physical laws. This is a very strong version of reductionism, then: generalisations in theoretical linguistics, taken to be about psychological states of affairs, must be reducible to physical laws. Indeed, this very position has been adopted by Botha (1979), as we will see. Before considering the implications of such a reductionism for theoretical linguistics, however, let us consider the problems of such a version of reductionism for psychology alone.

What Smart is saying is that there are no genuine laws of an explanatory sort in psychology, and the methodological objection to his position is that, if he is to reject phenomenalism, this means rejecting the reductionism it involves (see 1.2 on reductionism in phenomenalist philosophies of science). Consider the phenomenalist's reductionist position: it incorporates an assertion that we give epistemological priority to sense experiences, i.e. it takes these to be the only solid realities of which we can be absolutely certain. Since our knowledge of these is the only certain knowledge we may have, it follows for the phenomenalist that talk of anything over and above these involves a metaphysical leap not warranted by the phenomena. Generalisations concerning so-called 'realities' over and above the phenomena are taken to be reducible to statements about sense experiences. Thus, there are no generalisations about 'physical realities', only generalisations, of a truly explanatory sort, about sense experiences.

Considering that Smart rejects this position, it is rather odd that he proposes a remarkably similar approach to generalisations in biology and psychology. In Smart's case, we see a kind of epistemological priority being given to macroscopic physical realities (1963:16), which is extended to microscopic and submicroscopic realities. But the possibility that there may be realities over and above these, e.g. those of a biological and psychological sort, is ruled out, in much the same way that the phenomenalist rules out the possibility of physical realities over and above the phenomena. If the phenomenalist approach to submicroscopic realities is impoverished because it 'gives an ontological priority to everyday concepts (i.e. concepts relating to the macrophysical, such as "table", "door", etc.)' (p. 48), then surely Smart's own reductionism regarding biological and psychological phenomena is equally impoverished in giving ontological priority to everyday concepts of a physical sort. Interestingly, the 'metaphysical leap' that is required of the realist in assuming that there are physical realities (such as forces etc.) over and above the phenomena is very similar to the 'leap' required of the non-reductionist in assuming that there may be biological and psychological realities.

The appropriate response to this question of whether we ought to assume the existence of psychological realities relates to the methodological considerations discussed in 1.2: just as our realist assumptions about physical objects (and forces etc.) afford us a certain amount of heuristic gain, so assumptions about the existence of biological and psychological realities may similarly be heuristically fertile. If the objects, processes, and structures of a biological and psychological sort which we postulate do possess such heuristic fertility, then we are warranted in asserting of them that they are potential candidates for reality.

This would mean that we would allow that it makes as much sense to speak of there being states of mind, intentions, and memories in existence as it does to speak of there being stones, stars, and trees. Nor would we have to insist that propositions concerning states of mind be reducible to those concerning more primitive categories, any more than we would have to speak of propositions concerning stones being reducible to those concerning sense phenomena.

Thus, the objection to Smart's reductionism is of the same sort as the objection to phenomenalist reductionism, which Smart himself is opposed to.

Physicalist psychologism in linguistics

This kind of physical reductionism is adopted for linguistics by Botha (1979) in his 'progressive mentalism'. Botha rightly points out that Chomsky fails to 'specify in clear and precise terms the content of his expressions "to impute existence to theoretical constructs" and "to attribute psychological reality to theoretical constructs"' (1979:45), claiming that Chomskyan mentalistic claims are ontologically indeterminate. Given this observation, he outlines the basis for a physical mentalism, incorporating a set of conditions on the ontological status of linguistic entities, an essential one of which is his Physical Basis Condition, stated thus: 'A theoretically postulated mental entity cannot be granted existence unless it is somehow realised in the (physical) mechanism of the brain' (1979:64). He takes this a step further by proposing another ontological condition, the Neurological Condition: 'A mental entity postulated by a general linguistic theory cannot be granted existence unless certain neurons exhibit particular properties before they have been exposed to linguistic experience' (p. 66). This reflects a physicalism rather similar to Smart's and as such it reflects a lack of understanding of non-physicalist realism, such as Platonic realism. Thus, Botha assumes that Platonism is not a version of realism at all, but a kind of instrumentalism: 'a progressive mentalism [is distinct from] a nonmentalism such as Platonism whose claims are about fictitious, nonreal objects' (p. 61). This claim is simply false if Botha is claiming that Platonists do not claim real status for their ideal entities. Katz, for instance, makes the following statement: 'I now realise there was all along an alternative to both the American structuralists' and the

Chomskian conception of what grammars are theories of, namely the Platonic realist view that grammars are theories of abstract objects' (Katz 1981:3).

It is clear that 'ideal' in the Platonist sense is not the same as 'idealised'. An idealised theory is abstracted away from some set of phenomena; thus an idealised physical theory would utilise constructs whose properties are arrived at by abstracting away from actually encountered singular entities. An example of this would be frictionless planes, where we abstract, or factor out, certain properties of actually occurring planes and ignore others. With mental theories, we would single out certain relevant properties of mental phenomena and ignore others, the relevance being decided by the theoretical assumptions we make. However, such idealised constructs still relate to actually existing entities (theories referring to frictionless planes are still about actual spatiotemporal planes). Ideal (or 'abstract') entities of the Platonic sort, on the other hand, are not of this sort. Rather, they are taken to be real, but non-spatiotemporal, entities. In the Platonist's view, they are not fictions at all. Maintaining this distinction between ideal and idealised, we see that 'abstract' in the Platonic sense is parallel to 'ideal' and 'abstracted away from' parallel to 'idealised'. Botha notes this important distinction but makes the mistake of assuming that 'ideal' in the Platonistic sense means fictitious. It does not.

This point is important, as it undermines Botha's claims about the ontological status of the object of inquiry in theoretical linguistics. He states that 'No form of nonmentalism makes any claim about an underlying reality', and this forms the basis of his attempt to formulate an ontological 'import' for his progressive mentalism. The first condition he imposes on his progressive mentalism, the Reality Condition (Botha 1979:61), does not, as he supposes, demarcate Platonism from his version of mentalism. It is stated thus: 'In order for any form of mentalism to be progressive, its ontological claims must refer, ultimately, to entities which are both real and uniquely identifiable.' Botha mistakenly thinks that this condition draws a distinction between his progressive mentalism and Platonism. This is not the case, as we have seen, since Platonism is a version of realism which does in fact make ontological claims which refer to entities which are both real and uniquely identifiable. Of course, Botha could argue that there is no basis for assuming the existence of ideal, Platonic objects, but this is not what he has argued.

There are other methodological problems with the foundations of Botha's ontological proposals. One of these is the 'general metascientific perspective' (1979:66) from which he views these proposals. He states that 'The general tenet of such conditions [i.e. his ontological conditions] is the following: the existence or non-existence of a mental entity is reflected by the manner in which it does or does not interact with other kinds of entity or process which may be assumed to exist.' Botha quotes Dudley Shapere (1969) in stating the philosophical basis of his ontological conditions: 'To say that *A* exists implies ... that *A* can interact with other things that exist.' Botha then goes on to state that fictitious entities (which is what he takes Platonic objects to be) cannot interact with other existing entities.

This is mistaken, and in an interesting way: Botha cites as his methodological rationale the very rationale that Popper uses to support a position diametrically opposed to his. Popper cites the following argument to support his anti-reductionist proposals for a 'world three' which is ontologically distinct from the physical world:

One of my main theses is that World Three objects can be real ... not only in their World One [physical] materialisations or embodiments, but also in their World Three aspects. As World Three objects, they may induce men to produce other World Three objects and, thereby, to act on World One; and interaction with World One – even indirect interaction – I regard as a decisive argument for calling a thing real. (Popper & Eccles 1977:39)

We see here that the metascientific perspective that Botha thinks differentiates his physical reductionism from non-reductionist programmes is the very perspective that Popper uses to argue for a non-physicalist ontology. Thus, this metascientific perspective as a means of assessing whether an entity can be judged to be real can be used us a tool for arguing *against* physical reductionism. The upshot of all this is that neither Botha's metascientific perspective nor the specific ontological conditions he proposes are sufficient to rule out all non-reductionist ontologies.

Katz's Platonism (see 6.1) will be excluded by means of Botha's conditions, of course, since Katz's Platonic objects are said not to enter into causal relations with mental or physical realities, and this means that it is a principle of Katz's Platonism that interaction cannot occur. Those conditions will not, however, exclude either the autonomist metatheory given in chapter 2 or Itkonen's metatheory (5.1), and both of these are anti-reductionist.

A further methodological point to be made about Botha's reductionism is that his proposals do not accord well with the actual practice of theoretical linguistics. The discipline proceeds by means of linguists devising hypotheses and testing these against the data, which are arrived at by means of grammaticality judgements. This method has yielded interesting results and has not used neurological investigation either as its starting-point or as a point of reference for that matter. This suggests that it is a viable activity in itself, and that we need not refuse to assign real status to its constructs because of the absence of neurological correlates. No doubt the object investigated by theoretical linguistics interacts with, and is constrained by, neurological factors, in ways which we do not yet know, but this fact would be recognised, and investigated, in the sort of interactionist programme assumed here. By adopting interactionism, which allows for a strong autonomy thesis, we can successfully characterise the way that theoretical linguistics actually proceeds while allowing for interesting discoveries about the way in which neurological factors do come into play. The limitations of Botha's version of reductionism can be overcome in the sort of psychologism described by Fodor, and discussed in 4.3, in which a non-reductionist physicalism is adopted. But, before discussing this, I turn to a view of linguistic realities as psychological under a non-physicalist interpretation.

4.2   Dualism

Introduction

One of the most salient and widely discussed issues in the philosophy of mind is the question of whether mental processes and states (e.g. beliefs, intentions) are reducible to physical states of affairs, and the debate in which most of the arguments on this topic have been proposed is the one between physicalists, of varying sorts, and dualists. The mind/brain, or mind/body, debate, concerning as it does the question of whether properties that are attributed to mind are reducible to brain states and processes, is a long-standing and complex philosophical problem, and I make no attempt to contribute to it. It is relevant for our concerns here, though, since, in attempting to consider various differing versions of the view that the object of linguistic investigation is psychological in nature, one has to give a coherent account of what ontological import is carried by the expression 'psychological'.

If we are to consider non-physicalist accounts of psychological phenomena, the work of Descartes is as good a place to start as any, particularly since (a) the issues he tackled are relevant to any version of psychologism, and (b) his claims regarding innate ideas have played a central role in the philosophy of linguistics since Chomsky (1966).

Dualism and psychologism

There are two principal aspects to Descartes's philosophy which are important for this discussion: dualism and the doctrine of 'innate ideas'. Regarding the first of these, Descartes states, in the sixth meditation:

In this inquiry, what I first note is the great difference between mind and body, in that the body, from its very nature, is always divisible, and mind altogether indivisible. For truly, when I consider the mind, that is to say, myself in so far as I am a thinking thing, I can distinguish in myself no parts; I apprehend myself to be a thing single and entire ... The opposite holds in respect of a corporeal, i.e. extended, thing. (trans. Smith 1952:261)

In the next place, I take note that the mind is immediately affected, not by all parts of the body, but only by the brain, or rather perhaps only by one small part of it, viz. by that part in which the *sensus communis* is said to be.

Finally, I note that each of the motions that occur in the part of the brain by which the mind is immediately affected gives rise always to the one and the same sensation, and likewise note that we cannot wish for or imagine any better arrangement. (p. 262)

This partly states the basis of Descartes's dualism: mind is unextended whereas brain is extended; the two are qualitatively different and they interact in the sense that brain stimuli are registered as perceptions in the conscious mind, and conscious activities of the mind somehow get transmitted via the brain to the physical world. Of course, few are now willing to accept such a non-physicalist philosophy of mind, and perhaps the principal reason for this is that Descartes's philosophy was unable to explain how two such distinct entities are able to interact at all.

However, let us bear in mind the details of just how much of a non-physicalist interpretation of the mind Descartes had in discussing his proposals concerning innate ideas. On innateness, he states in the third meditation: 'To consider now the ideas, some appear to me to be innate, others adventitious, that is to say foreign to me and coming from without, and others to be made or invented by me' (trans. Smith 1952:216). In a reply to Regius concerning innate ideas, he writes:

I have never written, nor been of the option, that the mind needs innate ideas in the sense of something different from its faculty of thinking. I observed, however, that there were in myself certain thoughts that did not proceed from external objects, nor from a determination of my will, but only from the thinking faculty that is in me; and therefore, in order to distinguish the ideas or notions that are the content of these thoughts from other ideas which are adventitious or manufactured, I called them innate. (trans. Anscombe & Geach 1954:302)

However we regard Descartes's typology of ideas set out here, and regardless of whether his notion 'idea' was consistent (see Kenny 1967 for a critique of the notion 'idea' in Descartes's work), it is clear that innateness for Descartes is *mental* innateness, where 'mental' is interpreted as above, i.e. relating to 'thinking substance', unextended and distinct from brain process. This is important, since we cannot interpret what sort of innateness Descartes is proposing unless we first understand his dualist philosophy of mind. It is clear that it would be possible to posit an innate capacity of a purely physical, corporeal, extended sort; if we did, we would not be proposing the sort of innateness that Descartes was proposing.

What is equally clear is that, with regard to a specifically linguistic innate capacity, we must specify whether we are positing a physically or non-physically (as in Descartes) innate faculty. Any proponent of an innateness hypothesis must make it clear what form of the hypothesis he is proposing, that is, whether it is of the strictly Cartesian dualist sort, of a non-dualist sort, or of a kind neutral with regard to the dualist/physicalist debate.

The question which naturally arises here is whether Chomsky adopts a fully Cartesian innateness or not. Having done this, we can begin to establish what sort of psychologism Chomsky is proposing. It is as well, in trying to establish exactly what Chomsky is claiming, to trace Chomsky's thoughts on the matter chronologically, beginning with *Cartesian Linguistics* (1966). It should be emphasised that my concern here is not with the rationalist/empiricist debate but with the question of the nature of Chomsky's psychologism.

It is clear from his comments in *Cartesian Linguistics* that Chomsky appreciates Descartes's dualism. Early on in the work he states: 'Arguing from the presumed impossibility of a mechanistic explanation for the creative aspect of normal use of language, Descartes concludes that in addition to body it is necessary to attribute mind – a substance whose essence is thought – to other humans' (Chomsky 1966:5). He sums up Descartes's arguments concerning evidence from language in favour of mind as follows: 'In summary, it is the diversity of human behaviour, its appropriateness to new situations, and man's capacity to innovate – the creative aspect of language use providing the principal indication of this – that leads Descartes to attribute possession of mind to other humans, since he regards this capacity as beyond the limitations of any imaginable mechanism' (p. 6).

We can conclude thus far that Chomsky is at least aware of, and appears to accept, Descartes's conception of mind as non-corporeal. Later in the same work, he adopts the Cartesian notion of innateness as part of a universal grammar approach to language: 'By attributing such principles [the organising principles that make language learning possible] to the mind, as an innate property, it becomes possible to account for the quite obvious fact that the speaker of a language knows a great deal that he has not learned' (p. 60).

In *Language and Mind* (1968), Chomsky expounds the Cartesian idea of a *res cogitans*, a non-corporeal mind alongside body, and states that 'with all its gaps and deficiencies, it is an argument that must be taken seriously' (1968:7). However, having later argued against a purely behavioural approach to mental phenomena, he states:

On the other hand, the proposals of the Cartesians themselves were of no real substance; the phenomena in question are not explained satisfactorily by attributing them to an 'active principle' called 'mind', the properties of which are not developed in any coherent or comprehensive way.

It seems to me that the most hopeful approach today is to describe the phenomena of language and of mental activity as accurately as possible, to try to develop an abstract theoretical apparatus that will as far as possible account for these phenomena and reveal the principles of their organisation and functioning, without attempting, for the present, to relate the postulated mental structures and processes to any psychological mechanisms or to interpret mental function in terms of 'physical causes'. (1968:14)

I quote at length because it is clear from this that Chomsky appears to be adopting, not a Cartesian dualist account of innateness, but a 'neutral' account of the sort discussed in 4.3, where the physicalist/non-physicalist issue is left undecided or simply not addressed. I want to suggest that this be called the 'ontology-neutral' approach, but the term is, interestingly, not too appropriate for Chomsky, since his position is not entirely neutral. He does go as far as to claim that the reality under investigation is mental, and this constitutes the beginnings of an ontological interpretation of the object of inquiry. The problem is that he does not go on to specify exactly what we are to take 'mental' to mean. It is this fact which has given rise to much of the discussion concerning the content of Chomsky's claimed psychological status for grammars, and it is this which Botha rightly describes as the ontological indeterminacy of Chomsky's psychological reality.

The question of Chomsky's ontological assumptions becomes more complex if we consider the remarks in his later work. In *Reflections on Language* (1975), we find first the following statement, which corresponds to his position in *Language and Mind*: 'With the progress of science, we may come to know something of the physical representation of the grammar and the language faculty ... For the moment, we can only characterise the properties of grammars and of the language faculty in abstract terms' (p. 36). However, a later comment seems to suggest a non-neutral ontological position: 'Learning is primarily a matter of filling in detail within a structure that is innate. We depart from the tradition in several respects, specifically, in taking the "a priori system" to be biologically determined' (p. 39). For the present discussion, the departure from the Cartesian framework of assumptions is important; it is a definite indication that we are dealing with the 'biological' rather than with Descartes's *res cogitans*, the non-corporeal mind alongside body. And Chomsky explicitly recognises this departure from the Cartesian tradition.

So far, then, there are three different positions which Chomsky has to choose from: a strict Cartesian 'non-corporeal' innateness, a biologically interpreted one, or a neutral one. While he appears to have appreciated the nature of Descartes's innateness, he never explicitly adopts it. He does consistently state that our knowledge of physical instantiation is too underdeveloped to make any exact physical claims and that we must make do with abstract characterisations of cognitive structures. This position looks like a neutral one, but it is arguable (and Chomsky himself argues this, as we will see) that the biological view is not neutral with respect to the dualist/physicalist debate. The trouble for the dualist here is that 'physical representation' is ambiguous, given dualist assumptions. It may mean either (i) that our innate structure is entirely physical, but we are not at present in a position to say exactly what those physical structures are, or (ii) that the innate structure cannot be identified with the physical, but has physical correlates which again we are not in a position to specify.

As evidence that Chomsky's position is not a dualist one, consider the following statement in *Rules and Representations* (1980): 'For Descartes, mind is not a part of the biological world ... One might then argue that we are not studying Descartes's problem when we consider the human mind as a specific biological system, one with components and elements of varied kinds, to be explored as we would any other aspect of the physical world' (p. 30). This does suggest that the innate capacities Chomsky is interested in are decidedly within the physical side of the dualist's dichotomy. Thus, we must agree with Chomsky that he is not working within a Cartesian dualist framework. However, consider the following remark: 'This conclusion holds, however, only if we regard Descartes as an irrational dogmatist, that is, as putting forth doctrines that define the domain of inquiry, rather than as arguing for principles that he believed he had established within an inquiry more broadly construed. That seems to be a questionable move' (pp. 30–1).

This remark must be taken with rather a large pinch of scepticism; it is tempting to see Chomsky in this case as confusing Descartes with Chomsky. We cannot begin to revise what Descartes said in the light of how dogmatic we think he might have been about it, otherwise we end up with any number of interpretations of his philosophy. Consider whether we ought to avoid Descartes's innateness proposals altogether, along with the other basic principles of his philosophy, on the grounds that Descartes intended them in a non-dogmatic spirit. We may assume that Chomsky would rather object to that, and for much the same reasons that we should object to Chomsky's reinterpretation of Cartesian dualism. We have little alternative but to recognise that Descartes was a dualist (in fact, his is the classic dualist position) and to see Chomsky's proposals as a departure from Descartes. In doing so, we are hardly committed to seeing Descartes as an 'irrational dogmatist'.

That Chomsky is proposing a non-dualist ontology, and is thus departing from the Cartesian tradition is made evident in the following statement in *Rules and Representations*:

When I use terms such as 'mind', 'mental representation', 'mental computation', and the like, I am keeping to the level of abstract characterisation of the properties of certain physical mechanisms, as yet almost entirely unknown. There is no further ontological import to such references to mind or mental representations and acts ... the inquiry belongs to the study of mind, in the terminology that I will adopt, though it need in no sense imply the existence of entities removed from the physical world. (1980:5)

Since Descartes *was* asserting (and not merely implying) the existence of entities removed from the physical world, it is clear that this is a non-dualist position. Note, however, the cleverness of Chomsky's argumentative strategy in the succeeding paragraphs:

It is perhaps worth stressing, in this connection, that the notion of 'physical world' is open and evolving ... It may be that contemporary natural science already provides adequate principles for the understanding of mind. Or perhaps principles now unknown enter into the functioning of the human or animal minds, in which case the notion of 'physical body' must be extended, as has often happened in the past, to incorporate entities and principles of hitherto unrecognised character. Then so much of the so-called 'mind/body' problem will be solved, ... by invoking principles that seemed incomprehensible or even abhorrent to the scientific imagination of an earlier generation. (1980:6)

This does constitute a marked departure from the Cartesian tradition in that Chomsky is conceiving of shifting the very terms of reference in which Descartes framed the problem and his response to it. That is, if Descartes represents the classical dualist perspective on the mind/body problem, Chomsky is tackling it by assuming that the dichotomy itself be obviated, and thus the problem. This is a perfectly legitimate, not to mention interesting, approach to take to physicalist and non-physicalist philosophies of mind, but it cannot be construed as a continuation of Cartesian dualism: in fact, it contradicts it.

While speculative approaches to traditional philosophical problems are perfectly valid, we are left with much that is merely promissory in Chomsky's suggestion that we may come to understand, somehow, the nature of physical instantiation, to the point where we redefine the very notion 'physical'. One recalls Bloomfield's hope that the progress of physical science would somehow solve the problems of semantic analysis. Botha, too, hopes that neural discoveries will constitute the real referents for our theoretical terms, although his position is much more reductionistic than Chomsky's since Botha thinks that our current conceptions of 'the physical' will suffice, whereas Chomsky does not.

Botha, then, is clearly a physical reductionist whereas Chomsky appears to opt (finally!) for an 'ontology-neutral' position. However, I think I have shown that there are at least undertones of some sort of physical reductionism in Chomsky's proposals; I say 'some sort of' since with the indeterminacy that Botha mentions in Chomsky's ontology, it is hard to pin him down. In this connection, it is reasonable to suggest that the hint of physical reductionism in Chomsky's work is at odds with his longstanding position on behaviouristic reductionism. It is striking that Chomsky has long since championed the case against behaviouristic reductionism, and one might then expect him to take an anti-reductionistic position on the possibility of a physicalist reductionism in a psychologically interpreted theoretical linguistics. To the extent that Chomsky's position is (physically) reductionistic, it reflects a potential conflict, within his philosophy, on the question of reductionism in general. Of course, there is nothing like the naive reductionism of Skinner, with its impoverished ontology, in Chomsky's work, but so long as there is this ontological indeterminacy, we can accuse Chomsky of not having fully renounced reductionism.

It is interesting that at least one interpretation (Steinberg 1982) of Chomsky's philosophy takes it to be anti-physicalistic, which confirms the comments above (and Botha's) about the indeterminacy of his position and the subsequent scope for widely differing interpretations of it: 'Mentalists, such as Locke, Descartes, Putman, Chomsky, and the Gestalt psychologists would answer each of these questions [Do humans have non-physical minds, do these minds influence their behaviour, should the contents of these minds be studied in psychology and linguistics?] in the affirmative' (Steinberg 1982:89). We have seen that Chomsky cannot be said to have answered in the affirmative to the question 'Do humans have non-physical minds?' (nor can Putman, for that matter: see Putman 1982 for a statement to this effect), even though he can be said to have answered the other two of Steinberg's questions thus. The most interesting thing about this misinterpretation of Chomsky is that one might well expect an anti-behaviourist like Chomsky to oppose physical reductionism, which is presumably why Steinberg takes him to be a dualist.

In conclusion, we may say that Chomsky wants to avoid both dualism of the Cartesian sort and any reductionist physicalism of the Botha sort. The ontological indeterminacy of his position consists in his not actually coming up with anything in the way of coherent proposals for dealing with the dualist/physicalist problem, while at the same time failing to adopt an explicitly neutral view. I now want to look at the work of someone (Fodor) who has tried to avoid both of these positions.

4.3 Token physicalism

Fodor's alternative to naive reductionism

Fodor's approach to a psychological interpretation of linguistic realities is less radical in its rejection of reductionism than it might be, but it is more clearly articulated than Chomsky's and results in the development of a usable research programme. This fact is of particular significance if one stresses the importance of methodological, especially heuristic, factors in assessing the merits of philosophies of linguistics.

In his 1968 work, Fodor argues that one must distinguish between mentalist views in general and the strictly Cartesian view, of the sort discussed in 4.2, in particular. That is, he points out that a mentalism need not be of the Cartesian dualist sort, and that one could adopt a non-dualist mentalism without going to the behaviourist extreme of rejecting any and all mental phenomena as primary data for a theory of psychology. This is what we have been assuming; it represents a much more insightful view of the varieties of mentalism (what I have been calling psychologism) than that given, for instance, by Steinberg. This general approach is, arguably, much more interesting, and more likely to be fruitful, than the Smart/Botha reductionist one (recall that Smart explicitly rejects the idea that mental phenomena can count as primary data for theory of psychology).

Fodor is therefore attempting to propose an alternative to the two positions discussed in 4.1 and 4.2. In this sense, his is an attempt at an 'ontology-neutral' psychologism (bearing in mind the slight inappropriateness of this term in this context: there is an ontological position here, but the neutrality is with respect to the physicalist/dualist dichotomy).

In *The Language of Thought* (1975), Fodor outlines an alternative to both behavioural and physical reductionism. He points out that we can reject both the view that psychology should deal only with behaviour as its primary data and the view that we can only legitimately take 'inner' processes as primary data if they are assumed to be wholly physical. His approach relies heavily on the distinction between type (or kind) and token given in 2.4. Arguing against physiological reductionism, he claims that it is unlikely that every kind will turn out to be a physical kind, thus:

The reason it is unlikely that every kind corresponds to a physical kind is just that (a) interesting generalisations can often be made about events whose physical descriptions have nothing in common; (b) it is often the case that whether the physical descriptions of the events subsumed by such generalisations have anything in common is, in an obvious sense, entirely irrelevant to the truth of the generalisations, or to their interestingness, or to their degree of confirmation, or indeed, any of their epistemologically important properties; and (c) the special sciences are very much in the business of formulating generalisations of this kind. (Fodor 1975: 15)

In 2.4, I suggested that this set of observations is very important for linguistics as a special science. Observation (b) in particular is relevant to Botha's set of ontological conditions and Smart's comments about the status of generalisations in psychology. However, his ontological position differs from the interactionist one (with its strong autonomy thesis) which

I propose, as follows: Fodor argues against physical reductionism in psychology by arguing that 'the kind predicates of the special sciences cross-classify the physical natural kinds' (1975:25).

In adopting this argument, Fodor can oppose naive physiological reductionism by insisting that there may well be no one-to-one correspondence between psychological and neural structure, but rather a state of affairs in which psychological representations are correlated with neurological function, which is taken to cross-cut neural organisation. This frees us from the sort of requirement made by Botha, where specific neurons must be correlated with psychological (specifically, linguistic) entities. This is an improvement on Botha's set of proposals, but is not sufficiently removed from physicalism, if we assume that, within Fodor's framework, we are still dealing only with realities of a physical sort. That this assumption is justified is made clear by the following: 'Still, if mental events aren't to be reduced to behavioural events, what are we to say about their ontological status? I think it very likely that all of the organismic causes of behaviour are physiological, hence that mental events have true descriptions in the vocabulary of an ideally completed physiology' (Fodor 1975:9).

Fodor argues that this comment does not commit him to reductionism, because of the fact that he opposes type physicalism and proposes what he calls token physicalism. That is, psychological kinds or types cannot be expected to correspond to physical types or kinds, but psychological tokens may well be found to correspond to physical tokens. One could respond to this by observing that physicalism, even of the token variety, still incorporates the mistake of confusing objects of one ontological category (the physical) with those of another (the psychological). Such a confusion constitutes reductionism, even if it is of an indirect sort. However, Fodor's proposals do result in a research programme which is freed from any over-restrictive physiological constraints of the Botha sort, and is therefore *de facto* non-reductionistic. It may be argued that it is not therefore possible to distinguish in practice between a research programme based on Fodor's *de facto* anti-reductionism and a programme based on a radically anti-reductionist psychologism. Both would amount to a licence for an autonomous psychologically based linguistics (autonomous in relation to physiology or neurology).

But certain objections to his programme remain. Consider what Fodor makes of his fundamental assumptions. He wants to use them to establish the basis for a research programme which is freed from physiological restrictions and which rests upon the notion of computation as a metaphor for psychological processes, and representation as a fundamental part of the computation process. That is, he takes mental phenomena (decisions, surveying of options, etc.) as primary data for a theory of psychology rather than restricting the primary data to observable behaviour or physiological structure. This is perfectly justifiable: mental phenomena simply are the legitimate object of inquiry for the psychologist. It is equally justifiable, I suggest, to insist that the objects of linguistic inquiry are simply linguistic objects and their structure *per se*, rather than associated neural (or even psychological) phenomena.

It might appear that there is a contradiction in Fodor's position on reductionism, since he claims (1975:9), on the one hand, that the vocabulary of psychology is quite different from that of physics, but, on the other hand, that mental events have true descriptions in an 'ideally completed' physiology (p. 205). To establish whether there is a contradiction here, I consider his rejection of reductionism in detail. Attacking what he takes to be a strong version of reductionism, of the Smart variety, he cites (p. 10) the following representation of reductionist claims:

(1) $S_1x \rightarrow S_2y$
(2a) $S_1x \rightleftharpoons P_1x$
(2b) $S_2y \rightleftharpoons P_2y$
(3) $P_1x \rightarrow P_2y$

Here, (1) is to be interpreted as a law in a 'special science' (e.g. some non-natural science such as psychology, economics, or linguistics) which states, roughly, that 'all events which consist of x's being S_1 bring about events which consist of y's being S_2'. The formulae in (2) are taken to be bridge laws which contain predicates from both the special science to be reduced and the physical science (or lower-level science) to which the reduction is to be made. The formula in (3) is then the law in the reducing science to which law (1) is taken to have been reduced. It is then assumed that all the laws of the special science in question can be reduced in the same way to laws in the reducing science.

What Fodor does is to distinguish between reductionism of the classical sort and token physicalism, which he takes to be entailed by reductionism. The distinction is as follows: reductionism claims that there are natural kind predicates in an ideally completed physics and that these correspond to each and every natural kind predicate in any of the (ideally completed) special sciences. From this it follows that all events that are described by the laws of the special sciences are physical events. Fodor claims that one can accept the second of these components (all events are physical events) without accepting the first (correspondence of natural kind predicates between special and physical sciences). It is the conjunction of both components that counts as reductionism for Fodor, and the acceptance of the second one only that counts as token physicalism.

Recall (2.4) that Fodor achieves this separation of the two components by observing that a law in a special science could easily contain natural kind predicates for that science which do not correspond to natural kind predicates in a physical science, even if the statements in the special sciences can all be reduced to statements in the physical science. The example he gives is that of Gresham's Law in economics. If we assume that this law is valid, it tells us something about what happens in monetary exchanges under certain conditions. It may well be the case, Fodor admits, that every such event described by this law can also be described wholly within the vocabulary of a physical science: this is what constitutes his token physicalism. The rejection of type physicalism which he proposes in this example is as follows: while we may be able to formulate descriptions within a physical science of each and every event subsumed under Gresham's Law, the events so described are not likely to form a natural physical class. That is, the corresponding physical statements describing instantiations of Gresham's Law are not going to turn out to contain natural kind predicates.

That the latter observation is perfectly sensible is made clear if one considers the following example. Let us say that one monetary exchange is the exchanging of sheep, and another is the deletion of characters on a visual display unit (VDU) linked to a computer. It is rather obvious that it is not likely to turn out to be the case that these two physical events are included in some naturally occurring class statable under some physical law. Economic kinds, in short, are not likely to turn out to be physical kinds.

All of this seems unsurprising from a non-physicalist point of view such as Popper's or Itkonen's (5.1): it is unsurprising since economic systems are, in Popper's terminology, 'world three', not 'world one', objects. From an anti-physicalist position such as Itkonen's, acts of economic exchange are intentional actions (not spatiotemporal events), carried out on the basis of rules which are of a mutual knowledge sort, by conscious agents, and thus qualitatively distinct from the sorts of spatiotemporal events describable under the laws of physics. But this state of affairs is very damaging for the reductionist. Worse still for the reductionist, as Fodor points out (1975:15), is the fact that he must also postulate, in addition to apparently non-existent physical kinds, natural laws (of the bridge law sort) which will reduce the economic law to the supposed physical law. In my example, this means devising a law which will place sheep exchange and VDU operations within the same natural class!

It is in opposition to this untenable reductionism that Fodor introduces the idea of cross-classification of physical structures and entities by higher levels of organisation. What one winds up with at the level of the reducing science is a disjunction of predicates rather than a set of natural kind predicates. His diagrammatic exposition of this is given in fig. 1. This demonstrates the cross-cutting relationship between, say, economic processes and their physical instantiations, or equally between linguistic-as-psychological processes and their physical instantiations. It is clear from this that Fodor is committed to saying that psychological and economic processes can in fact be correlated with purely physical events, if in the cross-classifying way indicated. But this is to get matters the wrong way round. It has long been argued (this is Itkonen's point, for example, and Saussure's) that it is only *in virtue* of being linked to some economic or psychological (including linguistic) system that a physical event qualifies as being economic, or psychological or linguistic. Clearly, the significance (linguistic, economic, whatever) of a particular event is instantiated in the physical event, and thus there is an embodying of linguistic or economic form in substance, but one cannot possibly pick out physical properties of events which *constitute* the linguistic or economic significance in question.

One might argue that one *can* pick out specific phonetic properties of

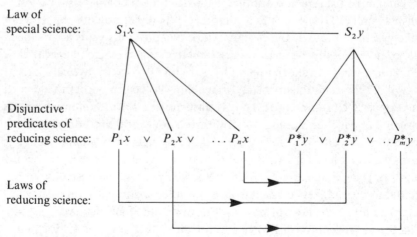

Law of special science: $S_1 x$ ———————— $S_2 y$

Disjunctive predicates of reducing science: $P_1 x \lor P_2 x \lor \ldots P_n x \quad P_1^* y \lor P_2^* y \lor ..P_m^* y$

Laws of reducing science:

Fig. 1.

acoustic or articulatory events which *do* bear formal (linguistic) significance, such as voicing or aspiration. But voicing, aspiration, etc., have no
meaning in themselves; they only have meaning *in virtue of the linguistic
system*: that is a valid Saussurean observation. And the system is not *constituted* by its substantive realisations, even if the system is *instantiated* in
the substance. Thus the system is not describable in terms of the properties
of the physical mode of instantiation. The token physicalist's attempt to
classify linguistic (economic etc.) systems and conventions as purely physical objects is, at the least, a difficult task, and is possibly also not a
requisite task for the explication of linguistic phenomena.

Physicalism, of any sort, thus appears to be untenable as a basis for a
psychologically interpreted theoretical linguistics. Whether some other
psychologically interpreted theoretical linguistics, which is radically non-
physicalist, can replace the sorts of psychologism discussed here is an
interesting question. It is interesting to note in this connection that it does
seem possible to obviate the dualist/physicalist debate in the philosophy of
mind *if* one avoids the psychological interpretation altogether. Thus
Katz's Platonism steers clear of the issue, and can afford to since the
object of inquiry, for him, is not psychological, and the problem of specifying what one means by 'psychological' does not therefore arise. Of
course, the Platonist is faced with a multitude of ontological problems
anyway, most of which are as difficult as the ones we have been looking at;
I will come to those below (6.1).

The question therefore arises whether we ought to characterise the
object of inquiry as psychological at all, and whether Fodor's version of
psychologism is compatible with the sort of autonomism given in 2.1.
Fodor's (1975) arguments in support of the validity of the notion 'private
language' allow for a speaker-internal mode of representation, and a
means of performing computations upon those representations. But, as we
observed in discussing Chomsky's response to Kripke, this neither undermines nor conflicts with Kripke's (or Itkonen's) arguments against the
purportedly private nature of linguistic knowledge. If Fodor's psychologism is interpreted as a means of specifying the ontological status of
linguistic objects, then it certainly is in conflict with the autonomism of
2.1. I suggest we interpret it as a means of specifying the nature of speaker-
internal computation upon a type of knowledge which is fundamentally
intersubjective, not in Pateman's (1987:67) distributive sense of being a
biological characteristic possessed by each member of a species, but in the
sense given in 2.1, where the reality of a linguistic state of affairs is fixed

intersubjectively. A question which is raised here concerns the nature of such a 'social' interpretation of linguistic knowledge; I turn to this question now, and try to show that such a view need not commit us either to the idea that linguistic knowledge is an object of social theory or to the view that such knowledge is constituted as a set of norms governing our actions.

5   *Linguistic objects as social realities*

5.1   Hermeneutics

Spatiotemporality and normativity

A non-psychologistic conception of linguistic objects as social reality is presented in Itkonen's (1978) *Grammatical Theory and Metascience* (henceforth *GTM*). In this and in *Causality in Linguistic Theory* (Itkonen 1983), Itkonen presents a fully developed philosophy of linguistics, of which I want to outline the principal arguments and assumptions. Itkonen's methodological position has already figured in our discussion: support for autonomism comes equally from the Popperian position given in chapter 2 and from Itkonen's hermeneutics, but support for a pragmatist interpretation of linguistic theories does not. I hope to show below that it is not only Itkonen's pragmatism which creates undesirable theoretical and metatheoretical consequences, but also his ontology.

A central set of distinctions is drawn in Itkonen's work between (i) spatiotemporal events, which are not intentional in nature, (ii) actions, which *are* intentional and are carried out by conscious agents, and (iii) socially agreed-upon norms, which constitute the basis for our rule-governed activities. This set of distinctions is important because it means, among other things, that grammatical inquiry is qualitatively distinct from physical inquiry. Physics has as its testing area spatiotemporal events, whereas grammar has as its testing ground intuitive reactions of native speakers, which are actions rather than spatiotemporal events (I will return to this below: its seems to me that it is, strictly speaking, the expressions one characterises as ill-formed or well-formed on the basis of these reactions, rather than the reactions themselves, which constitute the evidence in theoretical linguistics). Defining empirical sciences as those which are falsifiable on the basis of spatiotemporal occurrences, it follows from Itkonen that grammatical inquiry is a non-empirical science.

Two points ought to be made about this conclusion. First, it assumes that we take grammar to exclude psycholinguistics and sociolinguistics, which are both partly empirical (they both involve experimentation and corpus-based investigation, as in physics). Secondly, it assumes that Itkonen's definition of empiricalness should be accepted. Itkonen's statement that theoretical linguistics is not an empirical activity has, not surprisingly, generated a certain amount of hostility (see Dahl 1975, Linell 1976, and Sampson 1976 for some of this, and Itkonen's 1976 replies). I think we have to accept his distinction, which seems hard to deny; at the least, one would have to provide a theory of grammaticality judgements as spatiotemporal events to counter it.

However, one must distinguish between the validity of this methodological observation and the terminological matter of whether we do actually use the term 'empirical' for only the former of the two sorts of falsifiable activity. If we use 'empirical' for both, it would be useful to label them empirical$_1$ and empirical$_2$ to distinguish the two. Itkonen's use of the term 'science' for disciplines which are based on axiomatisation and 'empirical science' for that subset whose testing is spatiotemporal in nature seems as clear a decision about the terminological problem as any. And at least Itkonen has a clear conception of what he takes 'empirical' to mean, which is perhaps more than can be said for much current work in linguistics, where the expression is often used without its meaning being spelled out explicitly. One suspects that much of the heat in the reaction to Itkonen's use of the term comes from an assumption that any activity, to be scientific, must be empirical, i.e. an assumption which equates 'empirical' with 'testable'.

Connected with the above distinctions is the distinction between observable regularities (for instance, the regularities observable in the movements of planets and stars within a solar system) and spatiotemporal manifestations of social norms, i.e. patterns of observable behaviour which are rule-governed. It is clear that the former are properties of events whereas the latter are properties of actions. In the former case, there is no question of the observed regularities being correct in any sense, whereas correctness in the latter case is an essential part of the action. To take an example, the uttering of the following could not be counted as a potentially falsifying fact for our claims about tense-marking in English:

Maynard have be eats the spinach.

We simply disregard the fact that this has been uttered, on the grounds that it is 'incorrect' (in Itkonen's sense) and does not therefore even count in our attempt to falsify particular grammatical hypotheses, at least not if it is taken to represent a syntactically well-formed sentence of English. On the other hand, and in contradistinction to this case, no observable event in the solar system can be disregarded as being 'incorrect', since the term does not apply to physical phenomena (this is not to say that potentially falsifying observable events cannot be disregarded on other grounds).

I will not pursue the question of the status of the expression 'observable' in relation to 'events' here, though it is interesting to note that Itkonen's use of this fundamental distinction relies rather heavily on a systematic observation vs. theory distinction, which is rather disturbing, given the theory-laden nature of observation.

The notion 'correct' here might cause some concern, as perhaps does the claim that we can simply ignore much of the data in a recorded corpus on the grounds that it does not count as instantiating well-formed expressions in English. Itkonen has always allowed that there are non-clear cases when it comes to grammaticality, but claims that these do not impugn the status of the clear cases. I suggested in 2.6 that we make an even stronger claim than that: that there can be no notion of unclear cases or of 'asterisk fade' unless one has such a distinction; fading from a starred to a non-starred expression presupposes a starred vs. non-starred distinction. On the basis of the knowledge which allows us to make this crucial distinction, we are able to dispense with much of what is in a given corpus; it is clear that corpora play little or no part in strictly theoretical linguistics.

Itkonen further points out that, while it is clear that actions have a spatiotemporal aspect, it is not the case that they can be reduced to purely spatiotemporal events. This is true of our example about acts of monetary exchange in chapter 4: what constitutes an act of monetary exchange is not the physical events of, say, coins passing from one hand to another, but the underlying conceptual scheme which determines what will and what will not count correctly as a monetary exchange. Actions, then, are irreducible to events, and, furthermore, the norms which function as the basis for actions are not reducible to actions. Thus, if actions are characterised by the fact that they are carried out by conscious agents, and are therefore intentional in nature, as opposed to events, which are not, then intentionality and normativity are not reducible to ontologically more primitive factors.

This approach is hermeneutic in that it stresses the hermeneutic understanding we achieve in investigating our rule-based social actions as opposed to the observation we engage in when investigating spatio-temporal phenomena. While I wish explicitly to accept Itkonen's view of physical sciences as being qualitatively distinct from sciences such as theoretical linguistics, it is unfortunate, I think, to restrict the term 'understanding' to the knowledge we achieve in non-physical investigation; under almost any philosophy of science, it is uncontroversial to assume that we do in fact achieve understanding of the physical universe within the physical sciences.

Perhaps it is as well to mention another terminological point here. Hermeneutic sciences for Itkonen are opposed to physical sciences, and the term 'hermeneutic' is taken to characterise all those schools of thought in which a qualitative distinction is made between physical and human sciences. This he opposes to the 'positivistic' view which takes physical and human sciences to be methodologically parallel. Thus, Chomsky is a positivist under this scheme, whereas the approach to the methodology of theoretical linguistics adopted by Lass (see 3.3) is hermeneutic.

Itkonen's distinction between positivism and hermeneutics is likely to cause confusion since the term 'positivism' is widely used to refer to the sorts of philosophy of science proposed by the Vienna Circle, as discussed in chapter 3. Under this latter definition of positivism, Popper is clearly not a positivist, but a realist (we have seen, in 3.2, how his views differ from theirs), whereas, under Itkonen's definition, Popper *is* a positivist, since he adopts a version of methodological monism: he takes human and non-human sciences alike to be characterised by the same method. Itkonen is aware of this, and notes the problem in *GTM*; I mention it mainly to avoid confusion with terms discussed in earlier chapters, and to note an unfortunate terminological problem (though terminological problems are arguably rarely 'merely' so, and this is certainly true in this case: the explication of the terminological problems reveals interesting differences between Popper's, the Vienna Circle's, and Itkonen's philosophies of science).

It is clear that Itkonen wishes to see norms and actions as entirely social, rather than psychological, realities, thus: 'It is possible to abstract from every action the intentional element which, properly speaking, constitutes an action *qua* action. (This "intentional element" is to be understood, not as some psychical substance, but as a "pattern").' Furthermore, 'intentions, which are necessary constituents of actions, must be at least potentially conscious: to *do* something, one must be able to *know*, at least under some description, what one is doing. Thus knowledge is, in principle, inseparable from action ... knowledge is necessarily social' (*GTM*: 122–3, emphasis in original).

It should be stressed just how strong this claim is: that norms are not only socially established as the basis for our actions, but are entirely constituted by their social context. They constitute a kind of mutual knowledge, which he refers to as 'common knowledge', an intersubjective reality: 'Common knowledge literally constitutes concepts and rules as what they are, whereas their (social) existence is independent of the subjective knowledge of any individual person' (*GTM*: 322, n. 67).

This argument derives from his adoption of the Wittgensteinian argument against the possibility of private languages, discussed in 2.5; I will summarise Itkonen's statement of it now, as it is relevant to the social vs. psychological distinction which I am assuming.

First, he argues (*GTM*: 109–10) that there can be no concept of 'I' without the corresponding concepts of 'you', 'we', and 'he/she'. From this he concludes that an individual could not privately invent and follow a rule of language since, without the concept of others, the individual in question could not even have the concept of 'myself'. This appears to me to be fairly weak. Notice that Itkonen does not mention the concept 'it'. It is at least arguable that, even if one existed in a world without other people, one could acquire the concept 'myself' in contradistinction to the concept 'it' (relating to inanimate and animate, non-human, objects).

However, his second point is more convincing. Here he takes the case of someone's living in the public world and speaking an intersubjective language, but then attempting to invent a private language which is independent of any intersubjective language. Each term in this language would have to refer only to purely subjective experiences which are private to the individual in question, and which are therefore not susceptible to public identification. Itkonen makes the Wittgensteinian point that, if such experiences do exist, there is nothing that can be said about them, and that, if this is so, we cannot even begin to discuss the question whether we could devise a private language referring to them.

A third and final argument is cited by Itkonen against the possibility of private languages; I mention it only briefly as it strikes me as being rather unimpressive. Here he considers the objection raised above that one could conceivably have the concept 'myself' in a world where there are no other persons but only natural objects. His reply to this is that the concept 'myself' thus acquired would not in any way resemble our concept of person. But this is a rather circular reply: our concept of person is arrived at intersubjectively; any concept of person arrived at without reference to other persons is not really a concept of person because it is not arrived at intersubjectively. However, Itkonen does make the point that one could have no independent checks, in such a situation, on whether one was following a rule (of language) correctly. One would simply use a given linguistic expression in exactly the same way as one first used it, with the result that one could never manage to evolve the notion of correctness.

All of this is important for Itkonen because from it he concludes that rules of language are social rather than psychological realities. Among other things, this results in his rejecting the Chomskyan competence/ performance distinction, since knowledge of linguistic rules is inseparable from language use, and both are socially constituted. And, while he would not deny that we have some sort of internalised representation of linguistic rules, such rules are primarily objects of common knowledge rather than objects of a subjective, psychological nature. Thus, in Itkonen's view, Chomsky's position commits him to the existence of private languages.

We need to cite one further distinction of Itkonen's at this point, that between rule and rule-sentence: the term 'rule' may refer either to a socially constituted norm, outside of the grammarian's analysis and available to us by means of intuitive awareness, or to a statement in a grammarian's analysis of a language. The first of these is a rule in Itkonen's dichotomy, the latter a rule-sentence; the distinction is one between an atheoretical object (rule), which is normative in nature, an object of mutual knowledge, and a theoretical one (rule-sentence).

Some consequences of the hermeneutic position

Itkonen's account of the object of inquiry as fundamentally normative deserves serious consideration; I want to suggest, however, that he has not given good grounds for stating that it is indeed describable in this way. Consider, firstly, the status of sentences in his metatheory. It is clear that use is central to Itkonen's conception of language, and that speech actions constitute Itkonen's primary objects of inquiry:

According to this functional or pragmatic conception, the speech act is the primary unit of language. Within the speech act, one may go on to distinguish between the level of intersubjective interaction between speaker and hearer ... and the level of a reference to extra-theoretical reality ... The traditional concept of a 'sentence' proves to be a unit secondarily abstracted from the (primary) speech act. (*GTM*: 120)

In addition to this:

Sentences and types of speech act are equally normative entities: the former are concepts exemplified by utterances which in turn are results of act-tokens exemplifying the latter. Speech-act grammars analyse the concept 'correct (type of) speech act' just as sentence grammars analyse the concept 'correct sentence' ... Since sentence grammars are much more well-established than speech-act grammars, it is understandable that I shall concentrate on the former, in spite of the fact that they have just been shown to be logically secondary with respect to the latter. (*GTM*: 120)

Thus sentences do not play a particularly central role in Itkonen's scheme of things, and it is not clear that he need utilise the notion 'sentence' at all: once could easily dispense with it altogether and assume that the grammarian is engaged in formulating and then systematising rule-sentences which define 'correct speech-act type', whereby speech-act types are instantiated by speech-act tokens.[1] This is worrying because the construct 'sentence' does so much work in current grammatical frameworks, and is in fact a central part of the methodological basis of the generative enterprise: one would have to have very strong grounds for dispensing with it, or taking it to be of derivative status, as Itkonen does. When one considers that Itkonen takes his characterisation of AL to represent the tradition in grammatical inquiry, and that this tradition has been almost exclusively concerned with the sentence as an object of inquiry, one wonders just how close Itkonen's characterisation actually comes to mirroring what grammarians actually do.

One could reply that Itkonen allows that grammars are systematisations of sets of rule-sentences, and that his metatheory can therefore perfectly easily characterise the activities of theorists in AL. But consider the distinction between rule-sentences and grammars as systematisations of these. Take Itkonen's example rule-sentence ('In English, the article precedes the noun') as a statement of a linguistic norm. It is true that such a rule-sentence can easily be related to speech actions in the way that Itkonen describes: it is concerned with linear ordering, and our actions display temporal linearity in what Itkonen calls their spatiotemporal aspect.

There are serious problems, though, in maintaining the claim that what the rule-sentence describes is normative. Simple rule-sentences like this involve more than simply linearity. Consider why this rule-sentence is so uninformative (and allow that for Itkonen, it is meant to be so); it does not distinguish between immediate and non-immediate precedence, nor does it tell us anything about what elements may or may not intervene between the definite article and the noun, whether these intervening elements are more closely bound up with the noun or the article, what elements may follow the noun, how closely they are bound up with the noun and in what way, and how all of the elements preceding and following the noun (and we would be obliged to say 'head' noun) relate to the article. That is, all of the concerns of the grammarian need to be dealt with before we could turn the rule-sentence into an insightful statement about the language in question.

It is evident that, in attempting to improve on this rule-sentence, we need to appeal to notions such as function, constituency, hierarchicality, modification, complementation, and so forth. Just how these can be characterised as *normative* is not clear, and they would have to be for Itkonen's claims to stand. It will not do to say that such notions are part of some systematisation of rule-sentences, since rule-sentences *must* contain grammatical terms, and grammatical terms are defined by the grammatical theory they are contained within, which, of course, is what Itkonen insists on calling a 'systematisation of rule-sentences'. Itkonen gets it the wrong way round, surely: rather than the grammatical framework being built up as a systematisation of sets of rule-sentences, the grammatical framework is what *allows* us to frame descriptive statements of the rule-sentence sort in the first place. And, if the referents of the grammatical terms are not normative, rule-sentences cannot be about normative states of affairs. Whether such terms can be defined as conventions in a normative way remains to be seen; Itkonen has not done this. We can conclude that, even if rule-sentences describe purely normative objects, sets of these alone would be hopelessly insufficient as grammars.

This seems to me to be a fairly major defect in Itkonen's proposals: he *excludes* the objects of grammatical inquiry (sentences and their properties) in his philosophy of linguistics by claiming that the objects of inquiry are normative rules describable by means of rule-sentences. Itkonen is caught on the horns of a dilemma: if rule-sentences do not contain any theoretical (grammatical) terms, then they refer only to specific lexical terms, and are not general. They cannot therefore express rules. If rule-sentences do contain theoretical expressions, then the distinction between rule-sentence and systematisations of these dissolves (this latter consequence follows from the theory-laden nature of even the most low-level statement).

One means of escape from the dilemma is to appeal to the notion of analogy: rule-sentences should indeed contain no theoretical terms; rather, they should be expressed in terms of specific lexical items, and the speaker, in knowing these, extrapolates from them to other cases by analogy. This analogical strategy founders on the problems encountered by any attempt at explanation by analogy: we fail to characterise what it is that a speaker knows which allows analogical formation to occur. And that knowledge will have to be expressed in theoretical vocabulary. Thus, to allow that a speaker may know that the expression *Herbert is difficult to please* is well-formed by analogy with *Herbert is easy to please* will do nothing to explain what it is that the speaker knows in knowing this.

We saw in 2.5 that Chomsky (1986), like Fodor (1975), does indeed take himself to be committed to private rules and rule-following, and attempts to defend this view. Kripke's (1982) work shows that, in accepting that there is indeed a sceptical problem concerning private rule-following, we need not accept either a dispositionalist or behaviourist account of what it is to know and follow a rule. But we need not, in accepting the argument against private rules, be committed to Itkonen's use-based, normative account of rules and rule-following. We have yet to be shown that linguistic rules must be interpreted as normative in nature. The point that emerges is that acceptance of the argument against private languages need not commit us to a use-based or normative view of linguistic objects.

5.2   Languages as natural kinds and as objects of social theory

Psychologism and social realities

We have seen that Itkonen takes linguistic realities to be socially constituted in the sense of being the normative basis for our actions, and I have argued that this interpretation of linguistic objects as social realities is unpersuasive in that our account of the object of inquiry is theory-dependent, and the resulting theory-dependent linguistic notions we arrive at are not interpretable as norms. Itkonen's metatheory and the Popperian one I have given overlap inasmuch as they both entail autonomism and thus reject a purely psychological interpretation of linguistic objects, but what is at issue between them is whether the intersubjectivity of linguistic objects is of a normative sort.

One might argue that one can obviate the difficulties encountered by Itkonen's hermeneutics and at the same time capture the intersubjectivity of language without being committed to autonomism, if one allows simultaneously for the social constitution of linguistic objects as objects of mutual *belief* and for the existence of innately specified linguistic capacity (and thus linguistic knowledge which is primarily speaker-internal). It is this avenue which is explored and developed in Pateman (1987).

Pateman's general strategy involves, first, adopting a version of realism, based on the work of Roy Bhaskar (principally 1975 and 1979), which seeks to accommodate method in the social sciences to an overall philosophy of science by allowing that causal explanations may include reference to transfactually active mechanisms (Pateman 1987:25). These are mechanisms which are always active but for which constant conjunction of events cannot be required, since they may be said to be cancelled out on particular occasions such that they produce no effects.

Pateman then proceeds to show that, under this conception of science, the problems of Lass (1980) are obviated: we may indeed speak of explanation, even in the absence of the deductive–nomological form of explanation provided for the physical sciences. Bhaskar's point is that, even in the physical sciences, the D–N model is inadequate, since, in those sciences, one is dealing with open systems, rather than the causally closed world assumed by the D–N model. Thus, rather than arguing, as I have in 2.2, that deductive method may apply in the non-nomic domain of AL, Pateman argues that the domain is indeed nomic, but not in the traditional sense: it is our conception of causal law which needs revising, and, when this is done, we may still reasonably speak of causal laws, and thus causal explanations, in the social sciences, and in linguistics.

For Pateman, then, traditional modes of explanation in historical linguistics are interpretable as causal explanations: notions such as Humboldt's Universal are not undermined as explanatory devices, *pace* Lass, on the grounds that we cannot provide constant conjunction of events in their support. This view rather worries me. If we may allow for transfactually active mechanisms of this sort, what may count as counterevidence to the claim that they *are* active? That is, are claims about the operation of such laws falsifiable? I cannot see that they could be; that is, I cannot imagine what state of affairs could be specified which could count as falsifying evidence for the claim that Humboldt's Universal is an active mechanism in the evolution of languages. And, if this is so, the content of the claim is questionable.

Providing evidence which validates the notion (Pateman 1987: 37–9) is not to the point; what one wants is a conception of what would *invalidate* it. One suspects that no such conception is available. It is this property of falsifiability which characterises claims in the generative enterprise and marks them off from traditional analogical and functional explanations; we ought to be rather wary of abandoning it. Pateman is aware of, and explicitly acknowledges (1987:25), the problem of falsification with regard to the sorts of transfactually active and tendentially operating mechanisms he wants to appeal to. But his response to this is to fall back on criticism of 'simplistic Popperianism' and the impossibility of instant falsification. But we have seen (1.1) that this is to confuse falsification in principle with the question of how we respond to falsifying evidence. Tendency statements and claims about transfactually active mechanisms are, I am claiming, *unfalsifiable in principle*.

It is rather unfair of Itkonen (1988:552) to say that Bhaskar gives a 'grossly simplistic picture of current philosophy of science', but I do not think Bhaskar's observations about closed and open systems have the radical consequences he thinks they have. The Popperian realist need not conclude, from the fact that real-world experiments occur in artificially closed systems, that the physical world *is* a closed system. Rather, Popper acknowledges the fact that the physical world is an open system (see the comments from Popper in 2.3 above) without recourse to transfactually operating laws. Pateman's failure to note this reflects the fact that he adopts Bhaskar's philosophy of science without discussing its realist competitors in any depth, and speaks of it as if Bhaskar's were the *only* realist philosophy of science; we have seen that it is not.

These reservations aside, let us consider the nature of Pateman's objections to Itkonen's mutual-knowledge ontology and his proposals for an integration of nativism on the one hand and an account of languages as objects of social theory on the other. Pateman considers (1987:43–80) five different responses to the question 'what is a language', as follows:

(I) A language is a natural kind. (NATURALISM)
(II) A language is an abstract object. (PLATONISM)
(III) A language is a name given to a set of objects (for example, a set of grammars, lects or idiolects, characteristically taken to be properties of individual speakers). (NOMINALISM)
(IV) A language is a social fact, and that social fact is also a (or in a stronger version, the only) linguistic fact. (SOCIALISM)
(V) A language is a social fact, but that social fact is not a linguistic fact. (DUALISM, for want of a better word to indicate a view of reality as stratified and with at least 'weak' emergent properties) (pp. 44–5)

For Pateman, position I is valid, but this is rather obscured by his use of the expression 'a language' in place of 'language' here, since he is not in fact claiming that we may define a language as a natural kind, other than in the sense of Bickerton's (1981) 'ur-language'. Rather, he claims that languages are natural kinds in that they are 'distinguishable from other human or animal semiotic systems by essential, natural and replicable properties' (Pateman 1987:46). But it is surely language, the language faculty, rather than specific languages or languages considered generically which can be given this naturalist interpretation, and the traditional distinction between 'a language' and 'language' is surely important here, despite Pateman's claims (p. 46) to the contrary.

Pateman argues (pp. 57–72) that there are linguistic realities which are not socially constituted, utilising the arguments from first-generation creolisation and the 'home signing' systems of deaf children of hearing parents discussed in 2.5. His point is that it is reasonable to speak of privately invented rules of language, that these are linguistic realities, that they are not socially constituted, and that this counters any radical social interpretation of linguistic objects, such as Itkonen's.

He then seeks to sustain an interpretation of 'a language' which will allow that a language may be both a speaker-internal object of linguistic theory, and an object of social theory. He does this by allowing that objects such as 'English' are objects of mutual belief and are thus constituted as sociopolitical realities (Pateman 1987:75), and are best studied within a sociology of language (thus the view of languages as objects of social theory), and also by allowing that such beliefs are beliefs about the object of linguistic inquiry. It is this sense in which Pateman's ontology of languages is dualistic.

I want to suggest that Pateman is conflating two ontologically distinct objects here: languages$_1$, as objects of linguistic theory, and sociopolitically constituted languages$_2$, objects of social theory. These two objects may or may not interact in some specifiable way, but it is evident that, in seeking to devise an ontology which will cover *all* of our senses of the expressions 'language', 'a language', and 'languages', one is bound to end up with a pluralist ontology, since each of these terms denotes more than one sort of thing. But the ontology is pluralistic because the objects denoted by the term 'a language' are not subsumable under a single ontology, any more than the objects which are the referents of 'a bank' are subsumable under a single ontology.

Consider Pateman's point that '*S* believes, of the language$_i$ he speaks, that it is English' (1987:73), where the language$_i$ is the internalised object which the theoretical linguist is interested in. The attraction of this scheme to Pateman is that it allows him not only to claim that 'a language$_1$' maps partially on to 'a language$_2$', where the latter may be an object of conscious belief, but also to characterise the point at which this occurs. My objection to it concerns what it is for a speaker to believe that he speaks a language. We may say that *S* believes he speaks a language, that, parasitic upon this belief is the belief that the language is, say, Luxemburgish, and that other beliefs may also follow from the fundamental belief, for instance, that the language is not German. But I see no reason to assume that the belief that one speaks a language should be taken to be a belief about an object of theoretical linguistic inquiry, about 'a language$_1$'. I think that these sorts of belief are, rather, similar to the belief, for instance, that one is English: they are the beliefs that constitute one's sense of cultural identity, and as such are objects of social theory which simply do not impinge upon the goals of the theoretical linguist.

Thus, the theoretical linguist has, justifiably, nothing to say about propositions such as 'French is a beautiful and harmonious language, but German is an ugly and harsh one', which may well express beliefs of the sort Pateman describes. This is not simply because the expressions 'beautiful' and 'harsh' are not amenable to theoretical linguistic inquiry: whatever constitutes the referent of the subjects of these expressions, they are not languages in any sense which is relevant to the concerns of linguists. One may go even further and deny that the object of such beliefs, what is being described as beautiful or harsh here, is interpretable as a language in *any* coherent sense of the word (expressions such as these seem to me to be on a par with 'Ducks make a beautiful sound but geese make a harsh one').

I do not agree with Itkonen (1988) that Pateman 'has next to nothing to say about the data, i.e. about *language*, as this word is usually understood'; rather, my objection is that Pateman seeks an ontology which will fit with what may be said about 'a language' in *any* sense in which the term might be understood.

For Pateman, one of the advantages of his position is that it allows us to accommodate the fact that two speakers may agree that they speak the same language while disagreeing as to what it is (disagreeing on grammaticality judgements). Another is that we may change our beliefs as to what English is, and our ontology, he claims, must accommodate this too. These, and the other advantages Pateman cites (in connection with adequate characterisations of the phenomena of hypercorrection, standardisation, and prescriptivism), are all, interestingly, connected with sociolinguistic or purely sociological investigation, and not with linguistic theorising. This fact is unsurprising if they are indeed social and socio-linguistic phenomena.

One might reply that the first of Pateman's suggested advantages is not purely a matter of sociolinguistic concern, and that the position adopted in 2.2 faces a real problem in supplying a sense for the expression 'Modern Greek' in 'a generative grammar of Modern Greek'.[2] Given that I take 'a language$_1$' to be an abstract, intersubjectively real object, and that I take generative grammars to define such objects, it is not clear just how justi-fied we are in referring to a given grammar of this sort as a grammar of, say, Modern Greek. But I am also not certain that there is anything *at issue* when it comes to considering how justified we are in thus referring to them. We do not know, and do not require to know, whether there is any discrete or definable object which is the referent of such expressions: all we require is that there be an intersubjective state of affairs definable by the grammar; what community possesses this intersubjective knowledge need not be, and perhaps cannot be, specified.

Naturalism and the autonomy thesis

Consider now the question of whether autonomism is tenable in the light of Pateman's comments on nativism. In discussing the fourth answer to the question 'what is a language?' (sociologism: the view that a language is a social object and that this is also a linguistic object), Pateman cites Itkonen as a proponent of this view. It is certainly true that Itkonen is pro-posing that linguistic objects (specifically, rules of language) are social objects. And this view is fairly labelled sociologism, as long as we do not interpret this to mean that Itkonen takes linguistic investigation to be a form of empirical sociology. Given that this is reasonable, it is interesting to note Pateman's criticism of Itkonen's sociologism.

The principal line of argument that Pateman follows is this: Itkonen's 'linguistic objects as social objects' approach rests upon his adoption of and interpretation of the Wittgensteinian argument against private languages. If either the application of this to the methodology of theoret-ical linguistics or Itkonen's interpretation can be countered, then his sociologism can be countered.

Pateman attempts mostly to counter Itkonen's application of the private-language argument to theoretical linguistics, on the grounds that the conclusions Itkonen draws from Wittgenstein concerning grammatical inquiry are insupportable. Pateman's arguments relate, as we have seen (2.5), to the various issues raised by an innateness view of creolisation, second-language learning, and the signing systems developed by deaf children of hearing parents. What Pateman wants to do is to show that there is strong evidence for an innateness account of these, and that this is in conflict with Itkonen's anti-private-language thesis.

It is important that we bear in mind that Itkonen has never shown any aversion to the notion of an innately specified language-acquisition device, and has frequently stated that the innateness/anti-innateness debate is simply a debate about *how richly developed* innate specifications are. Itkonen's objection to Chomskyan linguistics is that 'it maintains a conception of language which is demonstrably equivalent to the private-language conception' (1978:113). Now, while it may be the case that Chomsky arrives at this private-language conception on the basis of his assumptions about innateness, it is not the innateness hypothesis itself which Itkonen is objecting to. Rather, it is the competence/performance distinction and the fact that Chomsky distinguishes knowledge from use. A defence of the innateness hypothesis need not, therefore, count against Itkonen's anti-private-language stance.

Pateman claims that there are two problems for Itkonen with regard to this supposed conflict between the innateness hypothesis and the anti-private-language position. First, he claims that 'if there are innate and other cognitive structures which can legitimately be talked about and theorised (e.g.in psycholinguistics), then there is the problem of determining the concepts which can legitimately be used in this enterprise, currently dominated by a computational paradigm in which concepts of "rules" and its cognates are central' (Pateman 1987:71–2). His point is that Itkonen must either accept that speaker-internal modes of computation ('the language of thought' in Fodor's sense) are private rules, or reply that such 'rules' are not rules in the relevant sense, and are thus irrelevant to the private-language question. This latter position is indeed Itkonen's. Pateman argues that this position is inconsistent with Itkonen's professed view that the Chomskyan conception of internalised language is tantamount to a private-language conception of rule-following. That is, Itkonen cannot have it both ways: the Chomskyan view either commits us to an argument for cognitive states describable as private rules or it commits us to an argument for cognitive states which are *in principle not describable* as private rules. Pateman's acute observations thus impale Itkonen, and autonomism, on the horns of a dilemma.

But Itkonen need not, I think, be caught in this dilemma. His point is that Chomsky is investigating public rules but misconstruing them as private states of affairs: Chomsky's conception is a private-language one, but his object is not the language of thought, the speaker-internal 'compiler' of linguistic input. Rather, Chomsky is in fact investigating the speaker-external language. Now this view can be maintained, I think, if we allow that what later become public rules may be invented privately, and that the rule-abduction capacity is speaker-internal, while the rules themselves are external. This is in fact the position I adopted in 2.5. Its viability will guarantee autonomism in the face of Pateman's objections (if it is not viable, then autonomism cannot, as far as I can see, be guaranteed).

The second purported problem for Itkonen concerns the nature of what he has achieved. Pateman argues that Itkonen (1978) is best seen as 'a contribution to the study of the social side of language' (Pateman 1987:72). That is, he claims that Itkonen has most probably 'theorised the domain of a discipline parallel to psycholinguistics – namely sociolinguistics' (p. 72). This is mistaken, I believe. It implies that Itkonen has constructed a metatheory for the social realities investigated under 'a language$_2$', the sorts of thing which Pateman takes to act as the objects of speaker belief. Itkonen has not done this, though; rather, he carefully distinguishes atheoretical rule and rule-sentence, corpus-based investigation in psycholinguistics and sociolinguistics as opposed to non-corpus-based grammars, and intersubjective rules of language vs. private inner states. It is not therefore possible to interpret Itkonen as having theorised sociolinguistics or 'the social side of language'. Itkonen's is a theory of AL; the problem with it is not its autonomism but its failure to allow us an interpretation of linguistic objects (sentences, their subparts, and their structure) as norms.

The upshot of this is that none of the arguments in favour of innately specified cognitive structures need undermine the notion that rules of language are speaker-external. Thus, this line of attack upon Itkonen, and upon autonomous linguistics, cannot proceed. AL is not abstractive linguistics, but abstract linguistics, linguistic theory which has abstract intersubjective objects as its object of inquiry. Now, Pateman concludes (1987:72) that there are linguistic facts which are not social facts, and that those facts are psychological rather than abstract. In response we may say that it is certainly clear that they are not social in Itkonen's normative sense or in Pateman's 'objects of belief' sense. But then Pateman's linguistic realities as social realities turn out not to be linguistic at all, and thus

Pateman is left, not with a dualism, but with straightforward psychologism.

We have seen (2.3) that linguistic realities are quite reasonably taken to be speaker-external, and thus not psychological in nature. The question arises whether linguistic objects, if not normative in nature, if not psychological, if not objects of speaker belief, may reasonably be given a Platonic interpretation. I hope to show in 6.1 that they may not.

6   Linguistic objects as abstract objective realities

6.1   Platonism

Katz's (1981) work *Language and Other Abstract Objects* constitutes a major departure from his earlier published views on the ontological status of linguistic objects. His paper 'Mentalism in linguistics' (1964), for example, argues for the sort of psychologism discussed in chapter 4. It is quite clear that Katz arrived at a Platonist philosophy of linguistics because of his interpretation of semantic representations in particular: his (1977) 'The real status of semantic representations' constitutes his first public statement of an overtly Platonist line on linguistic representation. And, it is arguable that, in this paper, Katz merely makes explicit what had been an immanent Platonism in his approach to semantics since his *Semantic Theory* (1972).[1]

However this may be, we can now take Katz, along with Postal, Langendoen, and other members of the 'New York School of Platonism' (see Langendoen & Postal 1984), to be the principal advocate of an explicitly non-psychologistic, non-social, ontology of linguistic objects, the details of which are as follows.

Katz adopts the tripartite distinction traditionally made in the philosophy of mathematics (and of logic), the nominalist/conceptualist/realist distinction. He argues that there have been two principal philosophies of linguistics in the twentieth century, namely nominalism and conceptualism. The first of these is reflected in the works of many of the American structuralist linguists whose work I described as instrumentalist in 3.1. He refers to it as being nominalist since, under this philosophy of linguistics, theoretical terms are no more than names and do not refer to extra-theoretical realities. What Katz calls conceptualism is the view that theoretical terms refer to mental entities. He takes this to characterise the Chomskyan position which I have called psychologism. Both of these are taken to be distinct from realism which, in Katz's view means Platonic

114

realism. In this respect, 'realism' here is not synonymous with what is referred to as 'realism' in the philosophy of science. Thus, under the latter use of the term, both Chomsky's and Katz's philosophies of linguistics are realist (albeit of very different sorts) whereas, in the former, only Katz's proposals are realist and not Chomsky's.

I do not want to pursue at length the matter of whether the trichotomy in the philosophy of mathematics and logic, or the realist/instrumentalist dichotomy in the philosophy of science is the most appropriate means of identifying positions in the philosophy of linguistics. However, it is noticeable that one's choice between the two appears to be at least partly determined by one's methodological and ontological assumptions about theoretical linguistics. The fact that Katz wants to identify theoretical linguistics as a discipline parallel in method to mathematics and logic, rather than the natural sciences, is reflected in his use of a philosophy of mathematics orientation. On the other hand, my use of a philosophy of science orientation might be taken to reflect the view that theoretical linguistics is a discipline parallel to those in the natural sciences. The choice of orientation thus begins to sound rather circular, that is, as if one's philosophy of linguistics determines how one is to go about talking about one's philosophy of linguistics.

While this may be the case for Katz (I do not argue that it is), I think the metatheory given in chapter 2 can be defended from the accusation of methodological circularity. My approach to the question 'Is the realist/instrumentalist debate relevant to the philosophy of linguistics?' is that we need to examine the issues raised in the debate and find out whether they help shed light on problems in the philosophy of linguistics. I think I have shown that they do. Thus, my adoption of a philosophy of science approach to the philosophy of linguistics does not necessarily presuppose a version of 'scientism' (what Itkonen calls positivism), otherwise known as methodological monism, the view that the method in the natural sciences parallels that in the human sciences. In order to establish whether theoretical linguistics adopts the same methods as the natural sciences or not, one must go into the methodological and ontological details, which is what I have done. I think I have established fairly clearly in what respects I take natural sciences to be parallel to theoretical linguistics, and in what respects they differ.

One further point needs to be made in this connection: it is mistaken, I think, to assume that these three positions (nominalism, conceptualism, and realism) encompass the entire range of twentieth-century philosophies of linguistics. I have already discussed such a philosophy which does not correspond to nominalism, conceptualism, or realism, namely Itkonen's mutual-knowledge anti-positivism. Saussure and Hjelmslev can also be interpreted as embracing none of these three. Indeed, one could be forgiven for assuming, on a reading of Katz's book, that the entire philosophy of linguistics in the twentieth century took place within the United States; his account takes Sapir, Bloomfield, Harris, and Chomsky to be the principal figures in this history, and excludes reference to Saussure. Hjelmslev is mentioned once, interestingly, as a possible forerunner of the sort of approach Katz takes. This is regrettable, as it leads Katz to assume, on several occasions, that Platonism is the only current alternative to nominalism and conceptualism, which it certainly is not.

Bearing this in mind, Katz's position can be identified by observing that he takes linguistic objects to be 'abstract' in nature, where 'abstract' means non-spatial, non-temporal, Platonic. Specifically, both sentences and languages (i.e. particular languages such as English) are abstract objects of a Platonic sort. A reminder here of a point I made in 4.1: 'abstract' for Katz is not equivalent to 'abstract' for Chomsky. Chomsky's object is spatiotemporal, and his representations of it are abstract in that they attempt to describe aspects of speakers' knowledge abstracted away from individual speakers and non-linguistic factors. Despite being thus abstract, Chomsky's representations are taken to be potentially descriptive of (or 'characterising') spatiotemporal entities and processes. Katz's abstract objects, on the other hand, are not spatiotemporal at all. One could equally use the terms 'ideal' in relation to Katz's objects and 'idealised' in relation to Chomsky's.

It should be mentioned at this point that Katz's ontology (of Platonic objects) is separable from his epistemology. That is, having established a case for Platonically real objects, Katz must erect an epistemology of how it is we come to have knowledge of such objects. This he does in the final chapter of the work (1981), but it is conceivable that Katz might abandon this epistemological framework and erect another which might fit his ontological assumptions better (of course, one may find it rather hard to conceive of what epistemology could possibly fit Platonism, but that is to anticipate).

Katz's arguments for taking the object of inquiry to be abstract objects are as follows. Knowledge of something is distinct from that which we have knowledge of. That is, the 'knowlege of' relation is a two-place predicate. If we accept that this is so, it is clear that our knowledge of the structure of a sentence is distinct from the structure of the sentence *per se*. It follows from this that sentences themselves, as the objects of our inquiry, are not competence units, are not units of knowledge, but are objects of which we have knowledge. In engaging in acts of intuition, we gain direct access to these objects; thus grammaticality judgements involve the accessing of linguistics objects *per se*, rather than some internal cognitive structure. Katz claims that, in this respect, linguistics is like mathematics and logic, which equally involve intuitive access to extra-psychological entities and relationships. His claim is that mathematical theory is a theory of numbers *per se*, rather than the human cognitive capacity for storing and processing representations of numbers. Likewise, logic involves the study of logical relations via intuitive judgements as to what are and are not valid inferences.

This interpretation of logic and mathematics is of course defensible, but is not universally accepted; to support it, Katz cites Frege and Husserl as proponents of such an interpretation of logic, and Hardy (1940) for this interpretation of mathematics. However, even if one were to argue that logic and mathematics are incorrectly construed as 'sciences of the intuition' in Katz's Platonistic sense, Katz could still argue for such an interpretation of theoretical linguistics. That is, Katz's Platonistic interpretation of grammatical inquiry is not dependent on the supposed parallel between it and mathematics and logic.

It is clear that intuition is thus distinct from psychological acts such as remembering, perceiving, and introspecting. While the latter might seem similar to the act of intuiting, in that both appear to be 'mental' acts in some sense, it is important to bear in mind that, for Katz, the object which one gains access to in an act of introspection is quite distinct from that which one accesses during intuition: one is an internal cognitive state of affairs, while the other is a non-subjective, and, for Katz, Platonic, object.

These considerations lead Katz to argue that theoretical linguistics is an autonomous science with respect to psychology, which he takes to include psycholinguistics. Being a science of the intuition, theoretical linguistics is not an empirical science at all, whereas psycholinguistics is. It is interesting that Katz does not give the same detailed consideration to the question of what is meant by 'empirical' as is given by Itkonen, but he does define empirical sciences as being about 'experience of the external world itself' (Katz 1981:23). While it is at least a reasonable approximation to say that the term means 'about experience', this is rather vague, in that acts of intuition are experiences of a sort. The notion 'external world' is of little help either, as mathematical and logical realities could well be said to constitute elements of the external world, even when interpreted Platonistically. However, since Katz takes Platonic realities to be non-spatiotemporal, it is as well to assume that in Katz's view empirical sciences relate to the spatiotemporal, or, in Itkonen's more precise formulation, are spatio-temporally falsifiable. Katz is right in arguing, as we have seen, that it is mistaken to equate 'empirical' with 'falsifiable', and that non-empirical (in this sense) theories may none the less be falsifiable.

In addition to these proposals, Katz argues that psychologism is both too restrictive and not sufficiently restrictive a framework for linguistic theorising. His arguments are as follows. Psychologism is too restrictive in that it takes linguistic objects to be psychological objects and thus constrains the class of possible grammars to those that happen to be compatible with the contingent facts concerning human cognitive make-up. That is, anything which happens to be a factor in the human cognitive machinery can potentially count as a factor in the grammatical description of a sentence (or, more generally, in the grammar of a language). Katz argues that this may often turn out to be undesirable. He cites the possibility that a set of grammars may contain all of the simplest grammars which 'predict and explain every grammatical fact about each sentence of English' (Katz 1981:86), but which are psychologically implausible, as opposed to a more complex grammar (i.e. notationally more complex or more complex in its set of rules) which is plausible psychologically. He points out that the conceptualist would have to choose the grammar which falls outside of our original set of economic and explanatorily successful grammars, simply because it fulfils our psychological criterion for the evaluation of grammars. Thus, it is possible, Katz claims, that our strictly methodological criteria (simplicity, generality, descriptive and explanatory adequacy) may clash with our general metatheoretical demand that grammars be psychologically plausible.

By the same token, Katz claims (1981:90–1) that such a requirement would be insufficiently restrictive in that it would not exclude from the class of permissible grammars those which are psychologically plausible but linguistically impoverished (i.e. which contain inelegant sets of rules which fail to capture significant generalisations).

Consider some of the objections one might have to these claims. The conceptualist may doubt that it is likely that we would end up with such a clash; that is, it is anticipated that simplicity, generality, etc. are themselves likely to be the basis upon which processing, storage, etc. take place.

Under this view, we take the methodological criteria to be not merely a set of principles for the construction of grammars, but a reflection of the principles underlying human cognitive make-up. Thus, both our grammar, as formulated by the linguist, and the object grammar function according to the same general principles, which of course is what psychologism is all about. The trouble with this objection to Katz is that it appears to fit badly with actual practice in theoretical linguistics. Considerations as to psychological plausibility rarely seem to figure in grammatical descriptions, and what linguists do seem to care about is the capturing of linguistic generalisations *per se*; it is thus perfectly easy to violate psychological plausibility while devising an elegant analysis. A case in point must be the emergence of transformational analyses during the heyday of the standard model, where such analyses were not guided by the desire to attain psychological plausibility, nor did they in fact satisfy any such desire. And yet such analyses were methodologically very appealing, and notions such as raising and extraposition still feature as descriptively useful constructs in much grammatical analysis (one still sees these constructs being used within more recent, non-transformational, grammar).

Consider another objection that might be raised by the conceptualist. It may be argued that it is vital to distinguish, in any theory of processing, between two or more logically equivalent grammars on the one hand and the set of possible modes of implementation of such grammars on the other. We might call these algorithms for grammars, by analogy with the computational distinction between a function to be computed and an algorithm or means of implementation for the computation of that function (say, in a particular program written in a particular programming language). Conceptualism does not require us, it might be argued, to reject a particular grammar just because some algorithm or other for that grammar is psychologically implausible.[2] The grammar is not equivalent to any particular algorithm and conceptualism could be said to require us only to adopt an *algorithm* which is plausible.

The most interesting facet of such an objection is that it incorporates a tripartite distinction between the following: a level of hardware, to be taken into account in any theory of processing, the algorithmic level, where a given grammar is made to work by means of a series of implementation instructions, and the level of the grammar itself, which is the level at which two or more grammars can be said to be logically equivalent (or not). The question that is begged by this set of distinctions is: what sort of thing is this highest-level object? If we take the human cognitive apparatus to contain a finite stock of hardware and a particular algorithm, or set of implementation instructions, then where does the internalised grammar fit in with these? And, if we allow that machines and/or alien species may possess differing algorithms for the same grammar in the cases where such beings/machines can decode a natural language, what is the status of the grammar for which they have distinct algorithms?

In anticipating this sort of objection by the conceptualist, Katz concludes (rightly, in my opinion) that, if the conceptualist adopts such a set of distinctions, he collapses conceptualism into autonomism. This is because it amounts to autonomism to allow a third ontological category distinct from the hardware and the algorithmic levels. Recall Fodor's token physicalism and its limitations (4.3): not only can we not expect grammatical kinds to turn out to correlate directly with algorithmic kinds, where the algorithm is some specific physical means of representing the grammar (type physicalism), but neither can we expect (physical) algorithmic tokens to correlate directly with grammatical tokens (token physicalism). This is because it is only by virtue of being a representation of a grammar that an algorithm has any meaning. We are compelled, therefore, to distinguish the grammar from both the algorithm and the hardware, and to allow that the grammar belongs to an ontic category distinct from either of these.

For Katz, this category is Platonic, thus:

There are also incompatibilities between aspects of the mental or neural structures in these various groups of creatures. We cannot abstract away from them without abstracting away from the psychological medium in which competences are realised and paying attention only to invariances across the range of cognitive systems that reflect the grammatical properties and relations of English sentences. Such abstraction would collapse conceptualism into Platonism. (1981:91)

While I agree with Katz that an attempt on the part of the conceptualist to distinguish grammars from their algorithms would collapse conceptualism into autonomism, I think Katz is mistaken in assuming that it is Platonism in particular, as a brand of autonomism, which would result from such an attempt. There is no reason why, having allowed that grammars are distinct from their modes of implementation, we need assume that they must therefore be Platonic in nature.

One of the principal problems with the notion that linguistic objects are Platonic concerns the possibility of our coming to have knowledge of such objects, that is, the question of supplying an epistemology to fit the ontological assumptions. Katz attempts to do just this in the final chapter of his book, where he assumes that intuition is fallible, that is, that our intuitive judgements may turn out to be mistaken. Katz does not consider that this weakens the role of intuition in Platonist linguistics, since he assumes that fallibility and certainty are properties of the knower rather than the known. Katz argues that it has been a mistake in the history of Platonism to draw an analogy between intuition on the one hand and both introspection and perception on the other, and to assume that intuition involves some kind of direct contact between the knower and the abstract object. This, he argues (1981:201), amounts to claiming that knowledge of abstract objects is knowledge by acquaintance. He believes that this is mistaken, because it is not possible for abstract objects, being atemporal and aspatial, to exert causal influences upon a knower: 'Being objective, abstract objects do not occur as a constituent of the conscious experience of a knower, and, being aspatial and atemporal, they cannot act on a knower through a causal process to produce a representation of themselves in the manner of sense perception' (Katz 1981:201). The immediate question this begs is that of how we can possibly come to have knowledge of these objects if they cannot act upon us to induce some representation, for it is quite clear that we do have such representations.

Katz answers this by proposing a Kantian epistemology whereby intuitive awareness is the effect of an 'internal construction'. That is, we internally construct intuitive judgements, and these either do or do not correspond to external abstract objects (thus fallible intuitionism). These internal constructions are therefore representations of abstract objects rather than abstract objects *per se*. The reader may by now be amazed that our internal constructions happen so often to correspond to external abstract objects. Katz responds to this by claiming that this apparently chance correspondence is not chance at all: we are endowed with an innately specified notion of 'abstract object' which 'specifies the ontological characteristics of the object that grammatical knowledge is knowledge of' (1981:205).

Katz thus transforms Chomskyan nativism into a native knowledge of 'abstract object'. None of this gives us any idea of how we are supposed to have come to possess such an innate knowledge, especially when one considers that abstract objects are not available for causal interaction during the evolutionary process. And this is the principal problem with Platonism: if we cannot in principle interact causally with Platonic objects, how can we know they exist? And how can we come to have knowledge of them? This is in marked contrast with my version of autonomism, which stresses interaction, and furthermore, following Popper (1972), uses the fact of interaction as *evidence* that it is coherent to talk of objective knowledge. Interactionism also assumes that the emergence of such a kind of knowledge is an evolutionary phenomenon.

Another interesting problem with Katz's philosophy of linguistics, which has been pointed out by Pateman (1983), concerns the conflict between his methodological criteria for the assessment of linguistic theories and his epistemological and ontological proposals. Katz adopts a simplicity criterion for the assessment of linguistic theories (Katz 1981:66–7, 234–7) and specifically urges us to adopt Occam's razor as a general principle of scientific methodology (p. 237). Now, given that Katz adopts a nativism akin to Chomsky's (but with knowledge of 'abstract object' as the innately endowed knowledge) in addition to an ontology of abstract objects, Pateman argues that Katz ought to apply his own simplicity principle and dispense with abstract objects, leaving us with straightforward Chomskyan innateness. Certainly, Occam's razor was devised precisely for this purpose (sometimes referred to as the trimming of 'Plato's beard': see Quine 1953:2).

Katz might, I suppose, argue that his simplicity criterion is a requirement for the assessment of linguistic theories and not metatheories, and that we cannot overcome the problems of psychologism without recognising the existence of Platonic abstract objects. While I am inclined to agree that we need to avoid the possibility of there being 'more in the world than there is in our ontology' just as much as we need to avoid the possibility of there being more in our ontology than there is in the world (Occam's view, and Quine's for that matter), I think that Katz must concede that his Platonic abstract objects are rather difficult to take seriously precisely because they are said not to be capable of entering into causal relations with human minds.

There is a further point that I want to make about Katz's abstract objects, concerning the question of what counts as a linguistic, and therefore Platonic, object. Katz argues that both sentences and particular languages count as objects of linguistic theory and are therefore subject to this Platonic interpretation. This is relatively controversial; while it is perfectly reasonable to assume that sentences are linguistic objects and thus susceptible to such a Platonic interpretation, it is rather novel to argue that particular languages (and, in principle, any and all future and past languages) should be taken to be objects of linguistic theory. The received view on this subject (Chomsky's) is that expressions like 'English' are best interpreted sociopolitically, such that 'English' is not a linguistic object, and it is a (linguistically) arbitrary matter whether Hindi and Urdu, for example, are or are not 'the same language'.

Katz, however, argues that such expressions do denote linguistic objects, which of course he interprets Platonistically:

claiming that notions like 'English', 'French', etc. and 'natural language' are not proper concepts of linguistics ... is like claiming that the concept of number is not a concept of mathematics, but a sociopolitical one (or that the concept of implication is not a logical concept but a sociopolitical one). (1981:79)

The claim that linguistic theories are not about psychological phenomena but straightforwardly about sentences and languages rests on the general epistemological distinction between knowledge that we have of something and the thing(s) that we have knowledge of. (p. 77)

I think that the first of these passages reflects a confusion. Quite apart from the fact that the concept 'natural language' is quite clearly a concept of linguistic theory, and quite different in status from concepts such as 'French', it is very clear that 'French' does not bear the same relation to linguistics as 'number' does to mathematics, or 'implication' to logic. The act of intuition, which Katz makes a great deal of, does not, for example, involve judgements about a language. It does involve judgements about sentences, however, and, if we then take such judgements to constitute the data and sentences to constitute the central objects of our inquiry, we can go on to characterise their properties and structure, yielding a whole set of objects within this domain such as 'constituent', 'syllable', 'complement', etc. While it is true to say that notions like 'sentence' are as much a central concept of linguistics as 'number' and 'implication' in mathematics and logic, it is not at all the case, as we saw in 5.2, that any linguistic theory need make reference to notions such as 'French'.

I believe that Katz is also mistaken, in the second of these passages, in utilising the 'knowledge of' relation to justify taking 'French' etc. as linguistic objects. He claims that what we have knowledge of are, not just sentences, but particular languages. One can take the knowledge of relation to have sentences and their properties as its object without having to make this claim. In having knowledge of a given set of sentences and their properties, or the grammar which underlies these, it is an arbitrary matter whether we refer to that grammar as 'French', 'Spanish', or whatever. Of course, part of the problem in discussing the notion 'a language' arises from the dual definition given for the term within the Chomskyan framework, where 'a language' is both 'a set of sentences' and 'a non-linguistic, sociopolitically defined entity'. Now, while this can cause confusion, there is not in fact any contradiction involved. One of these defines the object of inquiry, the other simply makes it clear that terms such as 'Japanese' have no explicit linguistic function. It matters not at all that once we have come up with a characterisation of what a speaker knows ('a language' in the formal sense: my 'a language$_1$'), we may not be able to decide whether this should be sociopolitically labelled as 'Dutch' or 'German'. Katz is therefore mistaken in making the following remark:

> Thus, we have to know from the outset what 'English' refers to in the characterisation 'the ideal speaker-hearer's knowledge of English'. The characterisation employs the term 'English' to specify the knowledge in question, just as the characterisation 'the ideal reasoner's knowledge of propositional logic' employs the term 'propositional logic' to specify the knowledge in question. (1981:80)

We have seen (5.2) that we do not have to know from the outset what 'English' refers to here, and we may conclude that the principal reasons for not taking Platonism to be a plausible ontology for linguistic objects are that it commits us to denying the highly plausible contentions (a) that human language is a product of the evolutionary process and (b) that there may be interaction between linguistic and non-linguistic domains.

6.2   Structuralism revisited

One interesting aspect of the Popperian objectivism I propose concerns Katz's 'knowledge of' relation. With the notion 'objective knowledge', we may reasonably speak of the object of linguistic inquiry as a kind of knowledge, as we do in the generative enterprise. To this extent, then, Popperian objectivist metatheory is 'mentalistic'. But, in adopting it, we assert that linguistic knowledge is crucially objective knowledge, intersubjectively constituted. Thus we propose a kind of 'external' status for linguistic objects, but not of the 'E-language' sort.

Now, structuralist linguistics, as we have seen (3.1) has typically not possessed the following three characterising properties of the generative enterprise: (1) A conception of the object of inquiry as a speaker-internal reality, (2) the notion that linguistic objects constitute a kind of knowledge, and (3) a definition of 'a language' as a set of sentences which are recursively enumerable. Structuralism has typically been divorced from the generative enterprise on at least these three counts. What I have sought to do is to show that a conception, as in (2), of linguistic objects as a kind of knowledge need not commit us to the psychologism of (1). But neither does it commit us to a rejection of (3). There is no need, therefore, to abandon generativity in adopting autonomism. And yet it is striking that autonomists tend either not to adopt generativity (Itkonen) or to move away from it (Lass, the New York School of Platonism: see Langendoen & Postal 1984).

It is of some interest, in this connection, to consider a recent reformulation by Lieb (1983, 1986: see also his forthcoming volume, *Prospects for a New Structuralism*) of the metatheoretical basis of structuralism in terms of the speaker-external nature of linguistic objects. Lieb (1986) argues, from the intentional, directed, nature of cognitive states, that linguistic objects must be the objects of cognitive states, and not cognitive states *per se*.

If we are to give an account of the way in which intentionality is present in speaking, knowing a language, and understanding speech, an account, that is, of linguistic intentionality, then we must, Lieb argues (1986:248–9), take linguistic objects to be speaker-external. Now, there are, as we have seen, different senses in which linguistic objects might be taken to be external, and one of these is the structuralist conception associated with Bloomfield, where they are external in being behavioural or substantive, in the sense of constituting articulatory or acoustic events. It is clear that this is not the kind of externality Lieb is talking about. He asserts (p. 249) that linguistic objects are abstract, in the sense that 'they are neither objects nor events in space–time but their ontological status is such that for each of them there is a specific ontological relation by which it is related to objects or events in space–time. Public accessibility also plays a crucial role in Lieb's metatheory: he asserts that the properties of linguistic objects must be publicly accessible, that brain states cannot be, and that linguistic objects and their properties must therefore be brain-external.

It is clearly of the utmost importance for Lieb's position that states of intending should not be reconstructable as brain states, and, in order to counter such an interpretation, he adopts Searle's (1983) theory of intentional states and actions. I have had little to say on intentionality; it is clearly central for both Itkonen and Lieb, and is linked with the framework of my Popperian metatheory at its foundations. Let us see why this is so.

Objectivism relies heavily on the notion that sentences are abstract intersubjective objects, and this commits us to a rigorous sentence/ utterance distinction, where sentences are not events but utterances are. Such a distinction requires, at some point, a theory of what it is to utter a sentence, and this is, no doubt, where intentionality must be appealed to.

But it would be false to say that the defence of the sentence/utterance distinction cannot proceed without such a theory; rather, it is something that one would hope, ideally, to be able to furnish. Unfamiliarity with the details of Searle's, and therefore Lieb's, theory means that it is unclear to me whether Lieb's account is the one that an autonomist generative enterprise requires. But there is, at any rate, a clear methodological defence of the sentence/utterance distinction (see Burton-Roberts 1985), showing that an abandonment of it, or a refusal to take it seriously, gets our linguistic descriptions into trouble.

For Lieb, linguistics, interpreted in a very broad sense, must be integrative: we must allow (1986:253) that there must be interaction between purely linguistic and extra-linguistic states of affairs, and in this sense his notion 'integration' is exactly the same as my 'interaction'. The non-necessary link between psychologism and the generative notion of providing a grammar as a definition of sentence for a language, where a language is taken to be a set of sentences, becomes apparent in Lieb's adopting a non-psychologistic, abstract ontology for linguistic objects which runs parallel to the Popperian one, while at the same time rejecting (Lieb 1983: 1–11) the fundamental generative conception of a language as a set of sentences. I offer some comments on Lieb's view of grammars and languages in Carr (forthcoming, a); for the moment, I want briefly to consider the prospects for a new interpretation of structuralism.

Lieb's (forthcoming, a) report on the Round Table concerning the 'Prospects for a new structuralism' at the fourteenth International Congress of Linguists (August 1987) claims new converts to the structuralist cause, notably: the recent typological work by Comrie and others, Katz's Platonism, Generalised Phrase Structure Grammar (GPSG), and 'Natural Morphology' of the sort proposed by Wurzel (1984). I am unable to comment on the last of these, but it should be clear that the link between work in GPSG and Katz's Platonism is very much a matter of ontology: there has been a clear lack of commitment to psychologism among those who contributed to work in GPSG. I will not seek to show that this is so; I understand that Uszkoreit (forthcoming) seeks to substantiate this claim. Thus two of the developments Lieb cites depart from the psychologism of the generative enterprise. Now, inasmuch as 'structuralism' can be interpreted as 'non-psychologistic', then these developments are towards structuralism. But one would have to allow that generative grammar, minus its psychologism, is a kind of structuralism, since GPSG is clearly generative. As to whether work in typology assumes a version of psychologism, I would have thought that this was so, but perhaps Lieb takes this work to be investigating linguistic objects in and of themselves.

What is quite clear is that work in typology does not proceed with the same methods as work in GPSG, and is clearly not a form of generative grammar. That is not to say that the two cannot be connected, but what does emerge from a brief consideration of Lieb's chosen areas is that the term 'structuralism' is being interpreted very broadly to cover any work that is not overtly psychologistic. Nor is there any reason not to include Chomskyan GB theory under this heading, since that work may effectively be divorced from its psychologistic interpretation, in the way that I have suggested. Clearly, what is required is a definition of what 'old' structuralism was about, so that we can gain a clear conception of the sense in which 'new' structuralism differs from it. I offer some comments on this in Carr (forthcoming, b); here, I suggest that the discussion of structuralist linguistics in relation to the realist/instrumentalist distinction, given in 3.2, along with its ontological consequences, might be a fruitful place to look.

What is striking about Lieb's ontological proposals is the extent to which they run parallel to Popperian objectivism. Perhaps Lieb is correct in suggesting that a new spirit of non-reductionism is gaining ground. What I want to do in the sections that follow is to consider some of the consequences for AL of the particular non-reductionist metatheory which I propose.

6.3   Objectivism and phonological realities

What is there to choose between the Popperian objectivist metatheory for linguistic inquiry given in chapter 2, incorporating the assumptions about reductionism and emergence that I have described, and a competing metatheory which is explicitly reductionist? Let us assume, uncontroversially, that we may reasonably require of any theory that it express significant generalisations about its domain in a maximally simple and perspicuous manner. This will allow us to evaluate competing theories. If we can then show that theories built upon a reductionist metatheory lose out in terms of generalising, and thus explanatory, power, then we may say that non-reductionist metatheories receive indirect support and are to be more highly valued than their reductionist competitors. I think that we can show this.

Consider the anti-reductionist interpretation of the relationship between phonological theory and general phonetic theory: it amounts to claiming that there are phonological generalisations which are not phonetic generalisations and therefore that there are phonological objects which are not phonetic objects. The language of phonetics, then, is necessary but not sufficient for the purpose of expressing significant generalisations. Against this, we can identify a position under which phonetics is both necessary and sufficient to the task. I will refer to this as phonetic reductionism or phoneticism.

To demonstrate the validity of the anti-phoneticist position, I will consider Natural Phonology (Donegan & Stampe 1979), Hooper's (1976) Natural Generative Phonology, and Ohala's metatheoretical claims about 'phonetic explanation' in phonology, all of which contain, in varying degrees, versions of phoneticism.[3] I then discuss Foley's (1977) proposals for a phonetics-independent phonology, which embodies the notion that the language of phonetics is neither necessary nor sufficient for the expressing of phonological generalisations.

First, then, Donegan and Stampe's (1979) proposals. They propose that explanation in phonology can only be achieved in terms of 'forces implicit in human vocalisation and perception' (p. 126), thus:

Natural Phonology properly excludes the topic of unmotivated and morphologically motivated alternations. Although these have often been lumped together with natural alternations in generative phonology, they *should* be excluded from phonology if it can, in principle, furnish no understanding of them. Of course, such alternations typically stem historically from phonetically motivated alternations, and these *are* in the province of phonological theory, as are the factors whereby the phonetic motivations were lost. The natural subject matter of explanatory theory includes all and only what the theory can, in principle, explain. In the case of natural phonology, this means everything that language owes to the fact that it is *spoken*. This includes far more than it excludes. Most topics which in conventional phonology have been viewed as sources of 'external evidence' are in the province of natural phonology as surely as the familiar matter of phonological descriptions. (pp. 127–8)

Donegan and Stampe tie these metatheoretical claims in with a hypothesis about the child's acquisition of phonological structure: that there are a set of 'natural' processes (e.g. word-final devoicing of obstruents) which the child will bring to bear on its language, but which may be 'suppressed' in response to the state of affairs in the language of its learning (e.g. the child may simply have to suppress the natural process of word-final devoicing, as in English).

Against this, we may argue that, if phonological theory is to include 'all and only what language owes to the fact that it is spoken', it is likely to be greatly impoverished as a result. Donegan and Stampe's discussion of the [s] : [z] alternation in German (as in [haus] : [hɔʏzə]) makes this clear. They adopt an anti-conventionalist approach to language, whereby it is seen as a 'natural reflection of the needs, capacities, and world of its users, rather than as a merely conventional institution' (Donegan & Stampe 1979:127). This enables them to single out the important and 'natural' fact that the [s] : [z] alternation is 'distinct in its nature, evolution, psychological status, and causality from the phonetically conventional aspects (of phonology)' (p. 127).

Donegan and Stampe overlook the fact that it is only by virtue of the fact that there is a phonological opposition between [s] and [z] in German that there can be said to be an alternation (as opposed to a free variation) between these; since this opposition is at the very least fairly largely conventional, I cannot see how Donegan and Stampe can avoid reference to conventionality in order to make any sense of the case they cite.

I accept, of course, that the voiced/voiceless distinction among consonants is hardly uncommon, and that it is a phonetic phenomenon which is natural in Donegan and Stampe's sense. However I think the limits of Donegan and Stampe's phoneticism are evident even where this extremely widely phonologised distinction is concerned. Rather simple cases such as the German alternations cannot be adequately explicated without reference to the conventional aspect of phonological alternations. And nor can the more complex, and more interesting, cases such as the (by now classic in the history of phonological theory) Russian devoicing rule, involving as it does a situation where there is an asymmetry in the system as far as the voiced/voiceless distinction in obstruents is concerned.

It is not clear to me how Donegan and Stampe are to account for the fact of this devoicing process. This asymmetry, whereby voicing is distinctive among one subset of the Russian obstruents but non-distinctive among another, exemplifies the conventional nature of phonological systems: in order to capture the nature of the devoicing process, it is essential that we demonstrate that it operates over both sets, such that we end up with two distinct consequences of the process, one in which 'phonetic overlapping' occurs and another in which it does not. This kind of naturalism presupposes the very conventionalism it seeks to avoid.

A rather less extremely phoneticist approach is adopted by Hooper (1976), and also by Venneman (1974 and elsewhere). Natural Generative Phonology (NGP) rests upon the supposition that the object of phonological theory is a speaker-internal reality (representations stored and

accessed by the speaker). Hooper makes specific claims about how the
speaker arrives at this representation, as follows: she claims that speakers
make generalisations across surface forms, i.e. from one surface form to
another, rather than from an underlying representation to a set of surface
forms. This is the essence of her True Generalisation Condition: 'all rules
express transparent surface generalisations, generalisations that are true
for all surface forms and that, furthermore, express the relation between
surface forms in the most direct manner possible ... the rules speakers formulate are based directly on surface forms ... these rules relate one surface
form to another, rather than relating underlying to surface form' (Hooper
1976:13).

Hooper takes this to be an important contribution towards constrain-
ing the notion 'possible rule' in phonology, since rules will not be of the
sort that relate underlying to surface forms. This would be a gain, of
course, assuming that one did not in the process diminish the explanatory
power of one's phonological theory. However, I think it can be shown that
this is precisely what happens.

Consider a particular case in which Hooper's principle is applied. She
proposes that the /e/ epenthesis phenomenon in Spanish is not describable
in terms of a *phonological* rule, since *all* surface sequences of /s/ + C are
preceded by /e/ in word-initial position: there is no alternation between
surface forms here over which a generalisation can be made, and there is
thus no methodological justification for a rule of /e/ epenthesis of the sort
Harris (1969) describes, thus:

$$\theta \rightarrow [e]/ \underline{\quad} s\,[+cons]$$

Her methodological position therefore forces her to abandon this as a
phonological rule of Spanish and to opt for an analysis whereby all the
esC-forms are entered *with* the epenthetic vowel in the lexicon. This leaves
Hooper with the problem of accounting for Spanish speakers' pronunci-
ation of foreign words with sC initial cluster. She achieves this by proposing a syllable structure constraint on Spanish which syllabifies sC clusters
with a syllable boundary between the /s/ and the C and inserts a V before
the /s/ (it is said to be 'preferred' for the epenthetic vowel to be inserted
before, rather than after, the /s/ since this allows the original order of Cs to
remain). Hooper's task is still not complete, however, since she is still left
with the problem of specifying the nature of the vowel insertion.

Hooper appeals here to one of two putative universal principles: (i) that
an epenthetic vowel must always be the 'minimal' (i.e. the weakest) one

and (ii) that it must be a V whose features are copied from a nearby segment (she does not specify how 'nearby' is defined, and her formalisation of this second principle fails to indicate what it means). She claims that Spanish utilises the first of these, on the basis of factors to do with 'the prosodic characteristics of the language'.[4]

The final analysis is still not accomplished, even after this amount of theoretical apparatus has been brought to bear on the problem: Hooper must still specify the precise quality of the epenthesised vowel. She does this by appealing to a language-specific strength scale for Spanish vowels, whereby /e/ is the weakest, and therefore the one to be inserted (in accordance with the principle mentioned above).

Now, quite apart from the clearly over-elaborate nature of this analysis in comparison with the traditional one, there is evidence that supports the traditional analysis. Harris has pointed out (1979:290–1) that allomorphs of the diminutive suffix vary according to the syllabic structure of their base forms, with /-θita/ occurring with bisyllabic bases and /-ita/ with bases consisting of more than two syllables (madre:madrecita vs. comadre:comadrita). He points out that /esC/ forms, which have a *phonetically* trisyllabic structure, pattern like bisyllabic forms (estudio:estudiecito, espacio:espaciecita, but *estudito, *espacito). This is evidence that the proper lexical representation for these forms is just as Harris's analysis would suggest: without epenthetic vowel.[5]

Thus, there do seem to be strong reasons for preferring the traditional (Harris-type) analysis over the Natural Generative Phonological one, and the metatheoretical implications of this are clear. The adoption of the sort of metatheory which Hooper proposes stresses the priority of (phonetic) substance over (phonological) form: 'A growing body of data shows that an interest in the way speakers analyse their language seems inevitably to lead to the study of substantive rather than formal principles of analysis, and substantive rather than purely structural evidence ... NGP is an appropriate framework for the study of substantive principles' (1976:106).

There is no reason why we should be forced to choose between a metatheory for phonological investigation which allows only for purely structural/formal evidence and analysis (Foley's is, as we shall see, and is consequently impoverished) and one which relies over-heavily on substantive principles of analysis (in the way that Hooper's does). Rather, an objectivist programme of the sort that I propose allows for the interaction of substance and form in a way that neither phoneticist nor abstractionist frameworks do.

Underlying NGP is Hooper's view that the object of analysis crucially relates to 'how speakers analyse their language'. I have suggested that a Popperian version of autonomism would allow for the possibility of dealing with linguistic objects *per se*, to a large extent independently of facts about speakers. This means that one need not be over-concerned with facts about speakers; at the very least, it is clear that Hooper's concern with the idea that speakers generalise over surface forms does not lead to noticeably better phonological analyses.

It might be argued that I have not attacked phoneticism at its strongest point, and, to deal with this possible objection, I want to consider Ohala's metatheoretical position on the relationship between phonetics and phonology. In his (1974) paper 'Phonetic explanation in phonology', he argues that the phonologist begins his task with 'sound patterns' and must then, if he is to be taken to be engaging in a scientific enterprise, seek to explain these. He may, of course, opt merely to construct a taxonomy and avoid the business of explanation.

However, science, claims Ohala, is essentially about explanation, and a scientific approach to the investigation of sound patterns would mean constructing an explanatory theory rather than a non-explanatory taxonomy. Ohala's argument is that much of the theory construction in modern phonology is taxonomy masquerading as theory. That is, Ohala says that the theoretical constructs devised and used by theoretical phonologists are lacking in 'empirical content' (1974:253) and therefore are to be taken to be mere labels with no explanatory force. Such theoreticians are therefore, Ohala argues, crypto-taxonomists. Since Ohala wants to engage in what he takes to be genuine explanation in phonology, he argues that phonologists must abandon such crypto-taxonomic labels and seek genuine explanations of phonological phenomena. These, he argues, are to be found in a wide variety of areas, but most notably in phonetics: it is 'one of the most important tools' (p. 270) we have in attempting to provide explanations for phonological phenomena.

Thus, his view of the relationship between phonetics and phonology is this: that phonetics is a subpart of phonology, and that phonological phenomena cannot be explained without reference to phonetic factors. To claim that phonetics is a distinct discipline from phonology is absurd, Ohala claims (p. 270, n. 3), since phonology is about explanation, and explanation in phonology is achieved principally by means of reference to phonetics. This view he takes to be in opposition to that expressed by Ladefoged (1971), who argues that a discipline must have a set of primitives which are defined outside of the theory in question, and that these primitives in phonology are provided by articulatory and acoustic phonetics, taken to constitute a domain outside of phonology proper.

Let us assess this in relation to a particular problem of analysis. In Ohala and Lorentz (1977), the analysis and status of labial-velars is discussed as a means of exemplifying the metatheoretical stance adopted by Ohala. Here, it is argued that constructs in theoretical phonology are not to be granted a realistic interpretation, that it does not make sense to speak of a phonological reality distinct from phonetic reality, and that explanation in phonology is only achieved when phonological statements are reduced to phonetic statements (which, I assume, are taken by Ohala and Lorentz to be interpreted realistically), thus: 'It is unnecessary to posit that the phonetic character of a segment differs from its phonological or "underlying" character unless the latter terms are defined in fairly innocuous ways' (1977:578). By 'innocuous', they mean definitions whereby terms in phonology are merely 'descriptively convenient' (p. 591), i.e. to be given an instrumental, rather than a realistic, interpretation. They distinguish between truly explanatory scientific theories and 'impressionistically-based, pre-theoretical taxonomies' (p. 577), associating phonological descriptions with the latter and phonetic ones with the former. They take the Sound Pattern of English (SPE) phonological framework to be an instance of such a pre-theoretical taxonomy which is awaiting proper 'scientific' reduction into the 'explanatory' terms of phonetics. The SPE treatment of labial-velars (in Chomsky & Halle 1968 and Anderson 1976, for instance) is thus seen by Ohala and Lorentz as mere taxonomic pigeon-holing; they suggest that a purely phonetic account of labial-velars would be truly explanatory.

Let us consider their proposed phonetic explanation. They take the acoustic properties of labial-velars to be the phonetic key to an explanation of their behaviour, as follows:

labials and back velars produce similar acoustic effects ... the explanation for this requires reference to the standing wave patterns of the resonant frequencies of the vocal tract ... the rule is: a construction at a velocity minimum raises the resonant frequency from what it would be for a uniform tube; a constriction at a velocity maximum lowers the resonant frequency from what it would be for a uniform tube ... [this] explains why a construction in either the labial or back velar position will have the similar acoustic effect of lowering the second formant and why simultaneous constrictions at both labial and velar regions will lower it even more. (Ohala & Lorentz 1977:582)

Taking this acoustic data combined with the articulatory and acoustic properties of nasals, they show that it will always turn out that labial-velars will behave like velars when it comes to nasal assimilation (we expect [nw] to assimilate to [ŋw] but not [mw], for instance). They then conclude, *contra* Anderson (1976), that labial-velars are not 'phonologic-ally' either labial or velar, but, as their phonetic description suggests, both labial and velar; they are unitary, not ambiguous, in character. Their func-tioning in some cases like velars and in other like labials can be explained either on the basis of purely phonetic data (as in the case of nasal assimila-tion) or on the basis of historical development, which itself is to be accounted for in terms of purely phonetic motivation of sound changes.

What Ohala and Lorentz especially object to in the 'mere pigeon-holing' of labial-velars into either a velar or a labial phonological category is the suggestion that a single phonetic phenomenon might be said to have variable systematic status in different languages (or, as we shall see, within a single language). In fact, Ohala disparages the idea of gaining insight into linguistic organisation by reference to linguistic systems: 'the be-haviour of speech sounds is better understood by reference to system-external factors than system-internal factors' (Ohala & Lorentz (1977:46).

Ohala allows that there may be straightforward acoustic phonetic accounts of why these behave as they do under nasal assimilation. I am perfectly happy to accept that this is indeed an explanation for the assimi-lation facts. It is parallel, but in acoustic terms, to the phonetic explana-tion as to why velars front before front vowels. I am also willing to accept that synchronic alternations between velar-like and labial-like behaviour of labial-velars (and between velars and palatals in my articulatory example) may well stem from such purely phonetically motivated states of affairs.

However, these purely phonetic phenomena (assimilations in this case) are rather dull in and of themselves, from a theoretical point of view. What is of linguistic interest is the effect such phenomena have on linguis-tic systems. Thus, a fronting of velars to palatal place of articulation can have interesting effects on the way the linguistic system is structured (and linguistic systems are real, as far as I am concerned). This is true, for in-stance, for French, where realisations of /k/ collapsed into realisations of /s/. Indeed, this sort of phenomenon (mergers, splits, in phonological systems) is part of the stock-in-trade of the historical phonologist. One does not doubt that, as Ohala points out, synchronic states of affairs can result from purely phonetically motivated processes, but it is the effect these have on a linguistic system that is of interest to the linguist. What we are dealing with in these cases is the interaction of form and substance, not the reduction of formal (systematic) states of affairs to substantive ones.

To illustrate this, consider Anderson's (1981) reply to Ohala. He cites data from Fula to show that we must postulate two distinct phonological segments underlying surface occurrences of the phonetic segment [w]. In stems with initial consonants which are continuants, there are alternations, in certain environments, which consist of prenasalised stops at the same place of articulation as the underlying continuant (he does not actually cite any other than the labial-velar, but I take it these are of the /l/→[nd] sort). The interesting cases are the alternants for underlying /w/. It turns out that these are of two different sorts, as follows:

(a) Underlying /war/ ('kill') has alternants [war] and [mbar].
(b) Underlying /war/ ('come') has alternants [war] and [ŋgar].

These two sets of alternants are symptomatic of the behaviour of two large sets of morphemes which consistently have labial, but not velar, alternants, as in the 'kill' morpheme, or velar, but not labial, alternants, as in the case of 'come'.

These data leave us with the rather evident phonological solution of distinguishing, within a single system, between two different labial-velars: one which we must represent as primarily a labial segment, and the other as primarily a velar one. The fact that there may have been a strictly phonetic motivation for this in the historical development of the language does not alter the synchronic fact that a single phonetic segment is phonologically ambiguous, rather than unitary.

There seems to me to be little methodological justification for interpreting the phonological analysis here as 'merely taxonomic pigeon-holing': we simply cannot give an adequate analysis of the data without reference to the constructs 'system' and 'systematic unit', and, according to the version of realism I adopt, this constitutes a satisfaction of the heuristic requirements for asserting the reality of a construct.

In asserting that these postulated phonological units are real, we are doing precisely what we do when we assert that phonetic constructs are to be interpreted realistically. To take an example, the construct 'wave', so crucial to acoustic phonetics, could be interpreted instrumentally as a kind of shorthand for a set of sense experiences and their properties in the Mach (1966) 'economy of expression' sense, but we are justified in interpreting it realistically in just the same way that we are justified in interpreting phonological constructs realistically: in terms of heuristic fertility.

We are therefore perfectly justified in speaking of distinct, if interacting, phonetic and phonological realities. We must reject phoneticism on the grounds that it forces us to adopt impoverished analyses and reject elegant analyses which capture interesting generalisations. Generalisations peculiar to a domain of inquiry, as we have seen (2.4), are what constitute that domain and its reality. Phonological realism is justified, and can be maintained while still allowing for the often complex ways in which phonetic and phonological realities interact.

The trouble with Foley's (1977) position is that it does not allow for such interaction. While Ohala thinks that theoretical constructs in phonology should not be interpreted realistically, and are to be reduced to acoustic and articulatory states of affairs, Foley's view is as follows: 'The basic phonological elements are defined not by physical acoustic or articulatory parameters, but rather by their participation in rules' (Foley 1977: Foreword). That he takes phonetic reductionism to be a methodological error is evident:

In the construction of a theory, the basic elements must be germane to the theory; just as the basic elements of a psychological theory must be psychological, so the basic elements of a phonological theory must be phonological elements. Chomsky & Halle, in attempting to create a phonological theory based on phonetic elements, consequently commit the reductionist error. A scientific linguistic theory would be based, not on physical properties of elements, but on abstract relations.

Conceptually we can recognise two types of features, phonological features, which refer to phonological relations, and phonetic features, which characterise the manifestations of the phonological units as sounds. (Foley 1977:5)

Foley cites the argument from the linguistic nature of systems which do not use speech sounds as their mode of manifestation to show that phonology is essentially not about speech sounds, but about relations between units in an abstract system. He takes *rules* to be the object of theoretical phonology, not speech sounds, and argues that a conflation of these two distinct realities constitutes an impoverishment of any theory of phonology.

Having made the entirely reasonable point that phonological realities are not phonetic realities, Foley isolates specific phonological elements and their phonetic realisations for discussion. He cites strengthening and weakening phenomena as evidence of phonological strength scales, and sees these as consisting of abstract phonological units, ordered according to their strength or weakness. Thus there is a scale which indicates propensity to spirantisation; this propensity is taken to be 'a manifestation of an abstract relation among phonological elements' (Foley 1977:28). The scale indicates that velars are the weakest category in relation to spirantisation propensity, followed by dentals, with labials as the strongest.

Foley then establishes a relation, which looks rather like a version of the sonority hierarchy and denotes the relation between, for instance, voiced stops and voiced continuants, the latter being weaker than the former. This is then followed by the citing of several other labelled relations concerning the phonological strengths among different phonological units.

It is difficult, even considering the nature of the elements mentioned so far, to escape the temptation to view these units and scales as being in some way tied in to phonetic factors. Spirantisation, for instance, typically occurs between vowels, whose articulation, with a stricture of open approximation, and whose typically voiced nature suggest a correlation between the environment in which spirantisation occurs and the articulatory properties of the affected segments. Voiced fricatives seem plausibly viewed as intermediate between voiced stops and vowels, in terms of degree of stricture, and the process whereby voiced stops spirantise looks overwhelmingly like a simple case of assimilation of degree of stricture. Articulatory versions of Foley's scale have been proposed (see Lass 1976 and Anderson & Ewen 1980 for suggested phonetically based interpretations of this scale) and are very feasible.

Foley, however, is obliged to treat this sort of scale as a purely formal scale demonstrating relations among entirely abstract phonological units, without any specific interpretation. On the question of the phonetic realisation of phonological unit, he claims (Foley 1977:48–9) that the same phonological elements receive different phonetic manifestations in different languages, but identical manifestations in a single language. However, to admit that this scale has a phonetic basis is not to commit the error of phonetic reductionism, but to allow for complex modes of interaction between phonological and phonetic realities. Thus, while spirantisation effects are themselves phonetically motivated, the effect of spirantisation on an abstract phonological system will depend on factors peculiar to the system in question. To quote Saussure (1959:142), 'the system, in other words, contains the seeds of its own evolution'.

It is interesting to note, finally, that both Ohala and Foley consider that the adoption of their respective methodologies would amount to assuring that the enterprise of constructing phonological theories is a truly scientific one. In Ohala's case, consideration of the realist/instrumentalist debate and its relevance for linguistic theory construction casts doubt on his conception of generative phonology as a pre-theoretical taxonomy. In Foley's case, there is no explicit statement of an ontological framework in which purely abstract phonological units are to be interpreted. With the adoption of a realist and interactionist methodology, I think we go some way towards characterising the nature of phonological inquiry, both in its methods and in the object of inquiry. It also seems to me that there are interesting observations about the nature of syntactic inquiry that emerge from this kind of autonomism.

6.4   Syntax and discourse

In this section I will make a few observations on the consequences of an interactionist methodology for the way we regard the relationship between syntax and discourse. Just as I argued against the reduction of phonology to phonetics, so I will argue that linguistic realities of a syntactic sort must not be confused with, and cannot be reduced to, facts about discourse, or communication in general.

This is in marked contrast to the position adopted by Givón (1984). His approach to the study of linguistic objects 'views data of language use, variation, development, behaviour, discourse processing and experimental cognitive psychology as part and parcel of one empirical complex' (p. 10). Givón takes the separation of linguistic systems from facts about the speaker, hearer, and communicative context to be only a necessary preliminary methodological step which, if practised (in the way it has been in generative linguistics), is 'bound to yield unsatisfactory results'.

That is, Givón is arguing, as I have, that one can evaluate a methodological framework in terms of the results of the theories it gives rise to. However, that is as far as we agree, since Givón assumes that the putting into practice of autonomism yields poor results in comparison with the adoption of what might be called a holistic methodology, where facts about, among other things, communicative function and general cognitive abilities are able to serve as explanatory devices.

I suggest that it is this holistic methodology which yields poor results. Far from assuming, as Givón does, that the division between theoretical linguistics and the general study of human behaviour and psychology is artificial, I propose that it is only such divisions that allow us to make any progress, and this, in accordance with the sort of realism I adopt, is sufficient reason for assuming that it is a reasonable guess at the way the object of inquiry actually is. Nor does this prevent my allowing that strictly linguistic states of affairs cannot be somehow tied in with facts about general cognitive abilities, communication, etc. What I want to maintain is that it is only through a non-holistic methodology, one where there are distinct but interacting domains, that we can make any headway; and, if this is so, that is our justification for saying that things really are the way our theories (and their accompanying metatheory) say they are.

This is exemplified in Givón's comments on the status of the investigation of sentences. The theoretical construct 'sentence' is at the very heart of all theorising about syntax in the generative framework. It is part of the foundations upon which generative syntactic theories are built; if they have allowed us insight into the nature of human language, then the 'sentence' construct has been crucial in our achieving what we have achieved. Yet Givón allows only that sentence grammars are a necessary methodological preliminary, and that, in practising sentence-level description and analysis, one must beware the danger of ignoring the 'semantic–functional correlates of syntactic structure' (1984:10). This danger can only be avoided if one proceeds to 'the next stage of syntactic investigation – the study of texts, and the study of the functional distribution of various morpho-syntactic structures within the text'.

With regard to this first stage, sentence-level analysis, Givón points out that it 'only tells the linguist that some structures are possible, may occur. It reveals nothing about the context and purpose of their occurrence, or how often they occur in comparison with other constructions that seemingly perform "the same" or similar function(s)' (1984:11). Thus, the linguist, to establish these things, must engage in quantification and statistical or probabilistic analysis.

Several comments are in order here. Givón assumes that sentences (he uses the term interchangeably with 'structures': I do not know what the metatheoretical status of 'structures' may be in his overall conception of the nature of linguistic inquiry) may or may not occur. It is not at all clear that they may. If these linguistic objects can be said to be real (I have argued that they *are* to be taken as real), then they cannot be viewed as spatiotemporally located events, as Itkonen rightly observes. But nor can they be argued to be acts (one cannot perform a sentence). That is, as Burton-Roberts (1985) makes clear, sentences are not the sorts of thing that may *happen*.

If this is so, then sentences cannot, by definition, occur in sequences in a text (this is simply a more restricted version of the more general claim that they cannot occur at all). And, naturally, one cannot determine their fre-

quency of occurrence. Nor does this mean that we take them to be
Platonic objects (I have explicitly rejected such a view), as Givón (1984:
12–13) assumes.[6] And this is the point (it is very much a metatheoretical
one) at which autonomists and holists, such as Givón, part company. I am
suggesting, therefore, that Givón is simply committing a category mistake
here, which is unfortunate, as it is located within the very foundations of
his metatheoretical position.

The autonomist need not be committed to a Platonic interpretation of
sentences: in order to avoid Platonism, it is incumbent upon him only to
show that sentences are not pre-existing objects, unavailable for causal
interaction with mental processes. We do this by showing that in syntax
there is something to be explicated; in order thus to understand and gain
insight into our object, it turns out to be essential to make a distinction
between sentences and the sorts of object that occur in texts, namely utterances. If this distinction is essential, that is our warrant in asserting the
reality of the two entities postulated. That the first of these, the sentence, is
not either a spatiotemporal event or an act is one of its defining properties:
it is this fact that causes us to want to make the distinction in the first
place.

This point is, to say the least, of great methodological importance: it is
at the heart of what the generative enterprise is all about (and it is Givón's
rejection of the sentence/utterance distinction as more than an expedient
preliminary that marks off his work as non-generative). It has recently
been made, very explicitly, by Burton-Roberts (1985) in relation to the
work of another non-generativist, Werth (1984), who shares many of
Givón's methodological predilections. Burton-Roberts points out some of
the confusions which arise if the sentence/utterance distinction is collapsed in the way that Givón and Werth have collapsed it. One ends up
with conceptually confused notions such as 'incomplete utterance', where
imcompleteness is predicated of utterances. But such a predication is
surely incoherent, Burton-Roberts says: every utterance is complete; it is
by virtue of their having a temporal beginning and end that they count as
spatiotemporal objects. As Burton-Roberts points out, the locution 'incomplete utterance' can only make sense if we interpret it as 'the (completed) utterance of a sentence fragment rather than a complete sentence'.
And, if we have to adopt the sentence/utterance distinction to make sense
of our object of inquiry, we are warranted in interpreting it realistically.

A parallel conclusion must be drawn from the attempt (on the part of
Lyons 1977, for instance) to predicate grammaticality of utterances.

Burton-Roberts argues that is it only in virtue of the 'sentence' construct that we can make any sense of utterances, and therefore of texts. I think that this point is parallel to the one I have been making about phonetic objects: speech sounds become an object of theoretical inquiry only in virtue of their relationship to phonological objects, which are not spatio-temporal. It is not mere 'artificial modularism', therefore, to draw a sharp ontological distinction between phonology and phonetics and between syntax and discourse; rather it is essential to the business of gaining insight into our object of inquiry. I think this becomes apparent when one considers modularist and holist issues when examining the relationship between theoretical linguistics and neighbouring disciplines.

6.5   Modularity and holism

A few comments are necessary, at this stage, on the sort of overall picture of the organisation of linguistic models which follows from the adoption of interactionism. I have said that its adoption supports the notion of an autonomous theoretical linguistics, and that this is crucially linked to the idea of autonomism within theoretical linguistics, to the modular picture of the organisation of a grammatical model containing descriptive devices for syntactic, semantic, and phonological phenomena.

It is clear that this kind of modular approach is most commonly countered by a different sort of metatheoretical approach in which modularity is abandoned, and some version of what might be called 'holism' is adopted. These two differing metaphysical research programmes might be summed up, rather superficially, as follows: modularism, interpreted realistically (in the way I want to interpret it) amounts to the claim that the object of inquiry is best characterised in terms of a set of discrete but interacting subparts, whereas holism typically incorporates the assumption that the notion of 'interaction between modules' is not a fruitful one. Just what a given holist wants to replace this idea with varies from one writer to another (and, very often, it is not clear precisely what conception of the organisation of linguistic objects and their structure the holist is proposing).

An interesting example of such an approach is that taken by Russell (1987a), who describes the notion of 'interaction' as 'promissory and pseudo-scientific' (p. 224). I try to show, here and in Carr (1987b), that the version of holism that Russell proposes leads to hypotheses that, at least as far as the explication of linguistic phenomena goes, are unfalsifiable (and therefore non-scientific). Thus, although it would be not quite accurate to say that holism itself (or at least Russell's version of it) is unscientific (it is a metaphysical research programme, not a theory, and is not in itself falsifiable), it would be accurate to say that, as a metatheoretical position, it does not lead to falsifiable hypotheses, and is therefore to be less highly valued than one which does. Of course, nor can one say that modularism is falsifiable itself, but one can point to the successes of falsifiable theories based upon the modular approach as evidence that it is to be more highly valued than holism.

Notice that modularism has tended to be embedded within what has come to be called the 'computational theory of thought' or the 'computation theory of the mind', in the sense in which Fodor (1975, 1983, and elsewhere) uses the expression. And it is the computational theory of thought, including modularism, that Russell is attacking.

A couple of points are in order here. The first is that one should really be speaking of the computational *meta* theory of thought, since this view of mental representations and processes is an overall picture, a metaphysical research programme, from which particular theories may be evolved. The second is that there is no *necessary* link between a broadly 'computational' metatheory and modularity. While it is evident that computational models can be devised on a modular basis, non-modular computational models are entirely feasible (see the work of Schank for this sort of non-modular computational approach to models of natural language understanding). It would be mistaken, therefore, to assume that arguments against modularism are necessarily arguments against a broadly computational theory of cognitive processes.

My response to the version of holism that Russell outlines might be termed the 'what else?' defence of modularism (to use a phrase of Dennett's). An example of a problem that Russell wants to deal with from a holistic point of view, or rather the syntactic problem which Russell claims is not a problem, syntactic or otherwise, is that dealt with in transformational work by means of the NP–Aux Inversion rule. Consider Russell's holistic response to the fact that the following is ungrammatical (Russell will not use the expressions 'grammatical' and 'ungrammatical', since he does not recognise either these or the construct 'sentence' to which they relate):

*Is the car which late will leave first?

Russell's comment on this is that 'action is hierarchical' and that one cannot 'lift the first occurrence of "is" out of a wh-clause to form an interrogative' for the same reason that one 'cannot release one's hand from a cup of hot coffee in order to position a saucer whilst returning the cup from the lips' (1987a:227). The former creates 'gibberish' while the latter creates a nasty accident. He says that there is some form of 'mental scaffolding' which ensures that the hand stays on the cup and the verb 'be' stays in the wh-clause; to quote Russell: 'things that belong together stay together'.

Thus the explanation Russell gives us for why verbs in some clauses (main clauses) can be inverted around their subjects and why others cannot is that the subordinate-clause verbs 'belong' in the subordinate clause. Why he restricts his attentions to 'wh-' subordinate clauses is unclear; the fact that the subordinate clause in question is of the 'wh-' sort is, of course, irrelevant. Russell's 'explanation' amounts to little more than asserting that one cannot invert verbs in some clauses because they cannot be inverted, but that we can invert verbs in others because they can be. If a verb in a subordinate clause 'belongs there', so do all the other parts of subordinate clauses. But we know that some of these can be moved (under extraposition, for instance), and we need a coherent theory of why this is so.

What is objectionable about Russell's metatheoretical position is the fact that he does not give us any indication of what exactly 'belonging' amounts to, and, with such vague and undefined notions, one cannot come up with falsifiable hypotheses. One must tackle hierarchicality, as a fairly clearly defined construct in linguistic theory, in a much more coherent way if one is to counter the claims made with it and about it in theoretical linguistics (or in its associated philosophical claims). My response to Russell's holism is therefore to say that, if this is holistic explanation, it leaves much to be desired, and, in the absence of a better articulated holism, we are as well to stick with modularism.[7]

If Russell's holism constitutes no real challenge to the idea of interaction between ontologically distinct domains, there are serious coherent accounts of hierarchicality which have been developed, and which might be considered to threaten the sort of interactionism I propose. The work of Simon (1981, for example) springs to mind; it is clear that in Simon's case we are dealing with a means of shedding light on the nature and origin of hierarchicality rather than constructing a vague 'things that belong together stay together' holism. Simon's proposals are best not described as holistic, and do not necessarily build a case for holism against modularism, but they may seem to undermine interactionism none the less. If, as he suggests, hierarchicality is likely to turn out to be a property of the internal structure (and, presumably, internal representations) of any complex organism, then it is seen not to be solely a property of specifically linguistic objects, and the idea of a linguistic, as opposed to a non-linguistic, capacity is in jeopardy.

It is not surprising, therefore, that Simon's work has been used to tackle the philosophical underpinnings of the Chomskyan innateness hypothesis, notably in Sampson (1978). While I have little to add to the rationalist/ empiricist debate, I should say that I do not think Popperian interaction-ism commits us to a version of the innateness hypothesis. Even if there is a good case for denying that humans are possessed of a specifically linguistic cognitive capacity, I am not claiming that the object of theoretical linguis-tic inquiry is of a mental (speaker-internal) sort, and the interaction I visualise is between speaker-internal states of affairs (innately endowed or otherwise) and specifically linguistic, speaker-external, objects such as sen-tences.

However, it remains to be seen whether such purely linguistic constructs as sentences will remain a valuable tool in linguistic research; I imagine that they will, since it is difficult to imagine a coherent linguistics without them. Moore and Carling's (1987) attempt at explicating what they call the 'problem of correspondence', for example, suffers precisely because it does not take the construct 'sentence' seriously as a notion that may be interpreted realistically. In an attempt to say what correspondence there may be between sentences as objects generated by the grammar and 'our everyday notion of sentence', they construct a sentoid/sentence distinction to distinguish between the former and the latter. But they give no idea of what our everyday notion of sentence is, and one cannot elevate this notion to the status of theoretical construct, as they do, simply because *it itself is in need of explication*. And this, of course, is precisely what the sentence/utterance distinction is designed to do (and will do if we take it seriously: see the remarks on Burton-Roberts and Lyons on p. 141 above).

The notion of linguistic realities in and of themselves is both coherent and indispensable; a picture of the relationship between them and non-linguistic, sociolinguistic, and psycholinguistic states of affairs will have to be formulated which recognises their existence. The principal threats I see to this sort of autonomism-plus-interaction come from work in Artificial Intelligence (AI) on the validity of modularism, but it is interesting to note, as a closing comment, that work in AI does not collapse cognitive psychology, theoretical linguistics, and computational modelling of cognitive processing (as the surveys in Thompson 1983, Biggs 1987, and Wilks 1987 show). There are clearly distinct AI problems, cognitive psychological problems, and theoretical linguistic problems, and much of the argumentation between AI, AL, and psycholinguistics researchers (as reported by Biggs 1987 and by Wilks 1987, for instance) centres around questions of the interrelationship between these disciplines. I think that an awareness that these fields are concerned with distinct, but interacting, domains, in the way that I suggest they are, can only shed light on what each discipline can and cannot achieve. As Biggs (1987:194) states, many of the problems one faces in understanding the relationships between these fields are metatheoretical; this is an observation I wholeheartedly agree with.

Concluding remarks

We live in a richly diverse world; it contains objects such as tables, benzene molecules, subordinate clauses, subatomic particles, morphemes, crossbills, and the Bank of England. It also contains the internal structure of each of these, and the relations between their subparts: stem–affix vowel dependencies, verb-agreement dependencies, exchange-rate fluctuations, magnetic attraction. The fact that benzene molecules, subordinate clauses, and the Bank of England are each of distinct ontological status does not undermine the fact that they are all objective realities: non-finite clauses are as real as tables, and just as objective. We cannot argue, from the nature of scientific inquiry, that we can be certain of the existence and structure of the benzene molecule but not of the nature and existence of linguistic objects. We cannot be certain that *either* of them exists or is the way we say it is. True, physical reality is somewhat more obliging at yielding its secrets to us than is linguistic reality, but that is largely a consequence of the fact that linguistic reality emerged as a part of our own evolution.

It may seem, on the face of it, that we have to choose between claiming that we are investigating a kind of knowledge in linguistics, and claiming that we are investigating speaker-external objects. What I have suggested is that the object of inquiry is both a kind of knowledge *and* a speaker-external reality: it is objective knowledge, which we can investigate by means of testable hypotheses yielded by the hypothetico-deductive method.

Notes

1 The case for realism

1 'Basic statements' is an expression used by Popper (1959) to cover what might be referred to as observational statements in a philosophy of science which proposes a distinction between observation and theory language. It reflects Popper's views on the theory-impregnated nature of observation in that he does not assume that statements of the form 'The oil is floating on the water' are theory-free. Popper allows that there is a large conventional element in such statements, and that they do not represent the sort of hard-core observational knowledge which instrumentalists such as the logical positivists assumed they did.

2 We will see below (2.1) that this is taken as an argument against the sort of realism I have been trying to sustain here. However, I will argue that it is a point in favour of, rather than against, realism.

3 The point that our theories are thus embedded is stressed by those, such as both Boyd and Hesse (1966), who view the background picture as a kind of metaphor; Boyd goes further in taking theories themselves to be a special kind of metaphor which allows us 'epistemic access' of the Quinean sort (see Boyd 1979), but adds to this a rather strong realist claim that such metaphors then 'cut the world at its joints', a position which reflects his belief that realism is 'an empirical hypothesis'.

4 To be fair to Kuhn, he has modified the extremely relativistic stance that seemed so salient in his *Structure of Scientific Revolutions* (1962) and has proposed (Kuhn 1976) a 'non-paradigmatic' rationality in an attempt to avoid the claim that there simply is no rational justification for scientific theories.

5 It has been pointed out to me (by Jim Hurford) that, if metascientific propositions such as scientific realism are empirical hypotheses, and therefore falsifiable, then we end up with the following contradiction: if we falsify scientific realism (as an empirical hypothesis) we have falsified a hypothesis which, by virtue of its being false, is said not to be falsifiable.

2 A realist philosophy of linguistics

1 This refers to an article first published in 1974 and reprinted in Fodor (1981). Page references here are to the 1986 reprint of Fodor (1981).

2 For a systematic distinction between 'introspective' and 'intuitive', which I accept, see 6.1 on Platonism.

3 Instrumentalism in linguistics

1 I agree with him. I do not have access to the unpublished manuscript which Lass refers to; however, I discuss Ohala's metatheoretical position in detail in 6.3.

2 Lass (personal communication) has pointed out that he has never claimed that autonomy presupposes instrumentalism, but has, rather, pointed out that it raises problems for positivist modes of explanation. His ontology of pure structure amounts, he says, to agnosticism over the realist/instrumentalist debate. He also says that his 'rational argumentation' is a kind of non-empirical testability, and that he is therefore not denying that there is a third choice between untestable theories and empirically testable ones. The trouble is, in my view, that agnosticism as to ontological commitment is instrumentalism by default: it is a withdrawal of the realist assumption. And rational argumentation, available in, for example, literary theory, is too weak a notion of testing to allow us to differentiate testing of linguistic theories from testing of literary ones. I agree with him that 'rational argumentation' covers testing in physics, linguistics, and literary theory, but believe that scientific testability marks off the first two of these from the last one.

3 For a discussion of how Popperian autonomism characterises the relationship between AL and historical linguistics, and on the notion 'analogical explanation', see Carr (forthcoming, a).

5 Linguistic objects as social realities

1 The expression 'speech act' here denotes any act of speaking, and its meaning is therefore more general here than it is in the literature on speech-act theory.

2 I am grateful to Hans-Heinrich Lieb and to Roger Lass for pointing out this objection; perhaps I can spell out my response this way: the objection turns on the meaning of the expression 'a language', such that, in asserting (i) '*X* speaks a language' and consequently (ii) 'that language is Flemish', we make a transition from one referent for the expression to another. It is therefore false, I am claiming, to say that the expression used to in (i) is co-referential with that in (ii).

6 Linguistic objects as abstract objective realities

1 I am grateful to Nöel Burton-Roberts for pointing this out to me; notice that it lends credence to the Popperian notion that our hypotheses may contain certain properties, such as contradictions, even if we as authors fail to perceive them. In this case, Katz's mentalism was contradicted by the Platonistic, non-mentalistic, nature of his view of semantic representation.

2 The expression 'algorithm for a grammar' may seem odd here. If so, perhaps I can explain what I mean by using another, very similar, computational analogy, used by Fodor (1983). One can distinguish between a function to be computed by some system, the *virtual* architecture of the system, which specifies the set of

instructions that need to be incorporated into a program to get the function to be computed, and the *physical* architecture of the program, which embodies these instructions. The level of virtual architecture here corresponds to the algorithmic level mentioned above. It seems to me that one can view linguistic systems and their realisations in precisely this way.

3 These are, of course, quite distinct theoretical frameworks, and I do not suggest that they amount to the same theoretical position. However, they all incorporate versions of phoneticism, as I will show.

4 Specifically, to do with the notion that Spanish is stress-timed and therefore has vowel weakening.

5 It may well be the case that one wants, counter to the spirit of the Sound Pattern of English (SPE) framework, to distinguish between morphologically orientated alternations and those which are motivated on a purely phonetic basis. Thus, a recent theoretical development, Lexical Phonology, as outlined in Kaisse and Shaw (1985), proposes a change in the way a model of phonological organisation represents these two sorts of alternation. However, the adoption of such a distinction need have no basis whatsoever in phoneticist metatheory, as indeed is the case with Lexical Phonology.

6 One of Givón's more peculiar claims is that Chomsky's interpretation of syntactic categories is Platonic. Note that his error here is similar to that made by Botha, discussed in 4.1.

7 The remainder of Russell's comments, on the realist assumptions inherent in my version of interactionism, are unworrying. This is because, in replying (in Russell 1987b) to the comments I make on realism in AL (in Carr 1987a), he mistakenly equates all versions of linguistic realism with Platonism, which I explicitly reject both there and in 6.1 above.

References

Adamska-Sałaciak, A. (1986) 'Teleological explanations in Diachronic Phonology'. Ph.D. thesis, Adam Mickiewicz University

Anderson, J. M. & C. J. Ewen (eds.) (1980) 'Studies in dependency phonology', *Ludwigsburg Studies in Language and Linguistics* 4

Anderson, S. R. (1976) 'On the description of multiply-articulated consonants', *Journal of Phonetics* 4: 17–27

(1981) 'Why phonology isn't natural', *Linguistic Inquiry* 12: 493–553

Árnason, K. (1980) *Quantity in Historical Phonology*. Cambridge: Cambridge University Press

Bhaskar, R. (1975) *A Realist Theory of Science*. Brighton: Harvester Press

(1979) *The Possibility of Naturalism*. Brighton: Harvester Press

Bickerton, D. (1981) *Roots of Language*. Ann Arbor: Karoma

Biggs, C. (1987) 'Chomsky and artificial intelligence', in Modgil, S. & C. Modgil (eds.) *Noam Chomsky: Consensus and Controversy*, pp. 185–95. Lewes: Falmer Press

Bloomfield, L. (1926) 'A set of postulates for a science of language', *Language* 2: 153–64

(1935) *Language*. London: Allen & Unwin

Botha, R. P. (1979) Methodological bases of a progressive mentalism, *Stellenbosch Papers in Linguistics* 3

Boyd, R. (1973) 'Realism, underdeterminism, and a causal theory of evidence', *Nous* 39: 205–49

(1979) 'Metaphor and theory change', in Ortony, A. (ed.) *Metaphor and Thought*, pp. 356–408, Cambridge: Cambridge University Press

Bresnan, J. (1978) 'A realistic transformational grammar', in Halle, M., J. Bresnan, & G. Miller (eds.) *Linguistic Theory and Psychological Reality*. London: MIT Press

Bresnan, J. *et al.* (eds.) (1982) *The Mental Representation of Grammatical Relations*. Cambridge, Mass.: MIT Press

Burton-Roberts, N. C. (1985) 'Utterance, relevance, and problems with text grammar', *Australian Journal of Linguistics* 5 (2): 285–96

(1986) *Analysing Sentences*. London: Longman

Carnap, R. P. (1937) *The Logical Syntax of Language*. London: Kegan Paul

Carr, P. (1987a) 'Psychologism in linguistics, and its alternatives', in Modgil, S. &

C. Modgil (eds.) *Noam Chomsky: Consensus and Controversy*, pp. 212–21. Lewes: Falmer Press

(1987b) 'Reply to Russell', in Modgil, S. & C. Modgil (eds.) *Noam Chomsky: Consensus and Controversy*, pp. 233–35. Lewes: Falmer Press

(1987c) 'Instrumentalism, realism, and the object of inquiry in theoretical linguistics'. Ph.D. thesis, Edinburgh University

(forthcoming, a) 'Autonomism, realism, and linguistic change', *Folia Linguistica Historica*

(forthcoming, b) 'An interactionist position', in Lieb, H. H. (ed.), *Prospects for a New Structuralism*. Amsterdam: Benjamins

Chomsky, N. A. (1966)   *Cartesian Linguistics*. New York: Harper & Row

(1968)   *Languages and Mind*. New York: Harcourt, Brace, & Jovanovich

(1975)   *Reflections on Language*. London: Temple Smith

(1980)   *Rules and Representations*. New York: Columbia University Press

(1982)   *The Generative Enterprise*. Dordrecht: Foris

(1986)   *Knowledge of Language*. New York: Praeger

Chomsky, N. A. & M. Halle (1968)   *The Sound Pattern of English*. New York: Harper & Row

Dahl, O. (1975) 'Is linguistics empirical? A critique of Esa Itkonen's *Linguistics and Metascience*', *Gothenburg Papers in Theoretical Linguistics*

Derwing. R. (1973)   *Transformational Grammar as a Theory of Language Acquisition*. Cambridge: Cambridge University Press

Descartes, R. *Meditations*, trans. Smith, N. V. (1952)   *Studies in Cartesian Philosophy*. New York: Russell & Russell

Meditations, trans. Anscombe, E. & P. Geach (1954)   *Descartes: Philosophical Writings*. Edinburgh: Nelson

Donegan, P. J. & D. Stampe (1979) 'The study of natural phonology', in Dinnsen, P. (ed.) *Current Approaches to Phonological Theory*, pp. 126–73. Bloomington: Indiana University Press

Duhem, P. (1953)   *The Aim and Structure of Physical Theory*. New York: Atheneum (first published in 1906)

(1969)   *To Save the Phenomena*. Chicago: University of Chicago Press (first published in 1908)

Eddington, A. S. (1927)   *The Nature of the Physical World*. London: Cambridge University Press

(1938)   *The Philosophy of Physical Science*. London: Cambridge University Press

Feyerabend, P. K. (1964) 'Realism and instrumentalism: comments on the logic of factual support', in Bunge, M. (ed.) *The Critical Approach to Science and Philosophy*, pp. 280–308. Cambridge: Cambridge University Press

(1975)   *Against Method*, London: Verso

Fodor, J. A. (1968)   *Psychological Explanation*. New York: Random House

(1975)   *The Language of Thought*. Hassocks, Sussex: Harvester Press

(1981)   *Representations*. Brighton, Sussex: Harvester Press (1986 reprint)

(1983)   *The Modularity of Mind: an Essay in Faculty Psychology*. Cambridge, Mass.: MIT Press

Foley, J. (1977)   *Foundations of Theoretical Phonology*. Cambridge: Cambridge University Press

Fraassen, D. van (1980)   *The Scientific Image*. Oxford: Clarendon Press

Givón, T. (1984)   *Syntax: a Functional-Typological Introduction*. Amsterdam: Benjamins

Hardy, G. H. (1940)   *A Mathematician's Apology*. London: Cambridge University Press

Harré, R. (1972)   *The Philosophies of Science*. Oxford University Press

Harris, J. W. (1969)   *Spanish Phonology*. Cambridge, Mass.: MIT Press
  (1979)   'Spanish vowel alternations, diacritic features, and the structure of the lexicon', in Kegl, P., G. Nash, & A. Zaenen (eds.) *Proceedings of the 7th Annual Meeting of the North Eastern Linguistics Society*, pp. 118–29. Chicago: University of Chicago Press

Harris, Z. (1963)   *Methods in Structural Linguistics*. Chicago: University of Chicago Press

Hempel, C. G. (1966)   *Philosophy of Natural Science*. Englewood Cliffs: Prentice-Hall

Hesse, M. B. (1966)   *Models and Analogues in Science*. Notre Dame: Notre Dame University Press

Heyting, A. (1962)   'After thirty years', in Nagel, E., P. Suppes, & A. Tarski (eds.) *Logic, Methodology and Philosophy of Science* pp. 194–7. Stanford: Stanford University Press

Hooper, J. B. (1976)   *An Introduction to Natural Generative Phonology*. New York: Academic Press

Hurford, J. R. (1988)   *Language and Number*. Oxford: Basil Blackwell

Itkonen, E. (1976)   *Linguistics and Empiricalness: Answers to Criticism*. Helsinki: University of Helsinki
  (1978)   *Grammatical Theory and Metascience*. Amsterdam: Benjamins
  (1983)   *Causality in Linguistic Theory*. London: Croom Helm
  (1988)   Review of Pateman (1987), in *Journal of Linguistics* 24 (2): 548–53

Jakobson, R. & M. Halle (1968)   'Phonology in relation to phonetics' (first published in 1956), in Malmberg, B. (ed.) *Manual of Phonetics*, pp. 42–59. Amsterdam: North-Holland

Joos, M. B. (ed.) (1958)   *Readings in Linguistics*. Chicago: University of Chicago Press

Kaisse, E. & P. Shaw (1985)   'On the theory of Lexical Phonology', *Phonology Yearbook* 2: 1–31

Katz, J. J. (1964)   'Mentalism in linguistics', *Language* 40: 124–37
  (1972)   *Semantic Theory*. New York: Harper & Row
  (1977)   'The real status of semantic representations', *Linguistics Inquiry* 8: 559–84
  (1981)   *Language and Other Abstract Objects*. Oxford: Blackwell

Kenny, A. (1967)   'Descartes on ideas', in Doney, W. (ed.) *Descartes*, pp. 227–49 Garden City: Anchor

Kimball, J. (1973)   'Seven principles of surface structure parsing in natural language', *Cognition* 2: 15–47

Kiparsky, P. (1982) 'From cyclical to lexical phonology', in van der Hulst, H. & N. Smith (eds.) *The Structure of Phonological Representations*, vol. 1, pp. 131–76. Dordrecht: Foris

Kripke, S. (1982) *Wittgenstein on Rules and Private Language*. Oxford: Blackwell

Kuhn, T. S. (1962) *The Structure of Scientific Revolutions*. Chicago: University of Chicago Press

(1976) 'Scientific revolutions as changes of world view', in Harding, S. (ed.) *Can Theories Be Refuted? Essays on the Duhem–Quine Thesis*, pp. 133–54. Dordrecht: Reidel

Ladefoged, P. (1971) *Preliminaries to Linguistic Phonetics*. Chicago: University of Chicago Press

Lakatos, I. (1970) 'The methodology of scientific research programmes', in Lakatos, I. & A. Musgrave (eds.) *Criticism and the Growth of Knowledge*, pp. 1–84. Cambridge: Cambridge University Press

(1978) *Philosophical Papers*, vol. 1. Cambridge: Cambridge University Press

Langendoen, D. T. & P. Postal (1984) *The Vastness of Natural Languages*. Oxford: Blackwell

Lass, R. (1976) 'On defining pseudo-features: some characteristic arguments for "tenseness"', in Lass, *English Phonology and Phonological Theory*. Cambridge: Cambridge University Press

(1980) *On Explaining Language Change*. Cambridge: Cambridge University Press

(1984) *Phonology*. Cambridge: Cambridge University Press

(1986) 'Conventionalism, invention, and "historical reality"', *Diachronica* 3 (1): 14–41

Lass, R. & J. M. Anderson (1975) *Old English Phonology*. Cambridge: Cambridge University Press

Laudan, L. (1977) *Progress and Its Problems*. Berkeley: University of California Press

Lieb, H. H. (1983) *Integrational Linguistics*, vol. 1. Amsterdam: Benjamins

(1986) 'Language is external – a reply to Helmut Schnelle', *Theoretical Linguistics* 13 (3): 239–55

(forthcoming, a) 'Report on Round Table 12: prospects for a new structuralism', *Proceedings of the 14th International Conference of Linguists*

(ed.) (forthcoming, b) *Prospects for a New Structuralism*. Amsterdam: Benjamins

Linell, P. (1976) 'Is linguistics an empirical science?', *Studia Linguistica* 30: 77–94

Luntley, M. (1982) 'Verification, perception, and theoretical entities', *Philosophical Quarterly* 32: 245–61

Lyons, J. (1977) *Semantics*. Cambridge: Cambridge University Press

Mach, E. (1966) *The Science of Mechanics*, Peru, Illinois: Open Court (first published in 1893)

Maxwell: G. (1962) 'The ontological status of theoretical entities', in Feigl, H. &

G. Maxwell (eds.) *Scientific Explanation, Space and Time*. Minneapolis: University of Minnesota Press

Miller, J. (1973) 'A note on so-called discovery procedures', *Foundations of Language* 10: 123–39

Mohanan, K. P. (1986)   *The Theory of Lexical Phonology*. Dordrecht: Reidel

Moore, T. & C. Carling (1987) 'Chomsky: consensus and controversy – introduction', in Modgil, S. & C. Modgil (eds.) *Noam Chomsky: Consensus and Controversy*, pp. 11–28. Lewes: Falmer Press

Musgrave, A. (1969) 'Impersonal knowledge'. Ph.D. thesis, University of London

Newton-Smith, W. (1978) 'The underdetermination of theory by data', *Aristotelian Society* 52 (suppl.), 71–91

   (1981)   *The Rationality of Science*. London: Routledge & Kegan Paul

Ohala, J. J. (1974) 'Phonetic explanation in phonology', in Bruck, A., B. La Galy & G. Fox (eds.) *Papers from the Parasession on Natural Phonology*. Chicago: Chicago Linguistics Society

Ohala, J. J. & J. Lorentz (1977) 'The story of [w]', *Proceedings of the 3rd Annual Meeting of the Berkeley Linguistics Society*, 577–99

Pateman, T. (1983)   Review of Katz (1981), in *Journal of Linguistics* 19: 282–4

   (1987)   *Language in Mind and Language in Society*. Oxford: Clarendon Press

Popper, K. R. (1959)   *The Logic of Scientific Discovery*. London: Hutchinson (first published in 1934)

   (1963)   *Conjectures and Refutations*, London: Routledge & Kegan Paul

   (1972)   *Objective Knowledge*. Oxford: Clarendon Press

   (1982/3)   *Postscript to the Logic of Scientific Discovery*, vols. 1 and 2 (1982), London: Hutchinson; vol. 3 (1983). Totowa, N.J.: Rowan & Littlefield (The content of these three volumes was written in the 1950s.)

Popper, K. R. & J. C. Eccles (1977)   *The Self and Its Brain*. Berlin: Springer

Putnam, H. (1962) 'What theories are not', in Nagel, E., P. Suppes, & A. Tarski (eds.) *Logic, Methodology and Philosophy of Science*, pp. 240–51. Stanford: Stanford University Press

   (1975)   'What is realism?', *Proceedings of the Aristotelian Society* 77: 177–94

   (1982)   'Three kinds of scientific realism', *Philosophical Quarterly* 32: 195–200

Quine, W. V. (1953) 'On what there is', in Benacerraf, P. (ed.) *From a Logical Point of View*, pp. 33–59. New York: Harper & Row

Radford, A. (1988)   *Transformational Syntax*. Cambridge: Cambridge University Press

Russell, B. (1908)   *The Problems of Philosophy*. Oxford: Clarendon Press

Russell, J. (1987a) 'Three kinds of question about modularity', in Modgil, S. & C. Modgil (eds.) *Noam Chomsky: Consensus and Controversy*, pp. 223–32. Lewes: Falmer Press

   (1987b)   'Reply to Carr:, in Modgil, S. & C. Modgil (eds.) *Noam Chomsky: Consensus and Controversy*, pp. 235–6. Lewes: Falmer Press

Sampson, G. (1976)   Review of Koerner (ed.) *The Transformational Paradigm and Modern Linguistic Theory*, in *Language* 52 (4): 961–5

(1978) 'Linguistic universals as evidence for empiricism', *Journal of Linguistics* 14: 183–206

Saussure, F. de (1959)   *Course in General Linguistics*, trans. Baskin, D., London: Owen (French edition first published in 1916)

Schlick, M. (1959) 'Positivism and realism' (first published in 1932), in Ayer, A. J. (ed.) *Logical Positivism*, pp. 82–107. Glencoe: Free Press

Searle, J. R. (1983)   *Intentionality: an Essay in the Philosophy of Mind*. Cambridge: Cambridge University Press

Shapere, D. (1969)   *Problems in the Philosophy of Science*. Oxford: Oxford University Press

Simon, H. (1981)   *The Architecture of Complexity*. Oxford: Oxford University Press

Smart, J. J. C. (1963) 'Materialism', *Journal of Philosophy* 60: 651–62

Steinberg: D. (1982) *Psycholinguistics*. London: Longman

Thompson, H. (1983) 'Natural language processing: a critical analysis of the structure of the field, with some implications for parsing', in Sparck Jones, K. & Y. Wilks (eds.) *Automatic Natural Language Parsing*, pp. 22–31. Chichester: Ellis Horwood

Twaddell, H. (1958) 'On defining the phoneme' (first published in 1935), in Joos, M. B. (ed.) *Readings in Linguistics*, pp. 55–80. Chicago: University of Chicago Press

Uszkoreit, H. (forthcoming)   'The status of linguistic objects in GPSG and other Unification Grammars', in Lieb, H. H. (ed.) *Prospects for a New Structuralism*. Amsterdam: Benjamins

Venneman, T. (1974) 'Phonetic concreteness in natural generative phonology', in Shuy, R. & C. J. Bailey (eds.) *Towards Tomorrow's Linguistics*, pp. 202–19. Washington, DC: Georgetown University Press

Werth, P. (1984)   *Focus, Coherence, and Emphasis*. London: Croom Helm

Wilks, Y. (1987) 'Bad metaphors: Chomsky and artificial intelligence', in Modgil, S. & C. Modgil (eds.) *Noam Chomsky: Consensus and Controversy*, pp. 197–206. Lewes: Falmer Press

Worrall, J. (1982) 'Scientific realism and scientific change', *Philosophical Quarterly* 32: 201–31

Index